I0816565

SACRED WINE

SACRED WINE

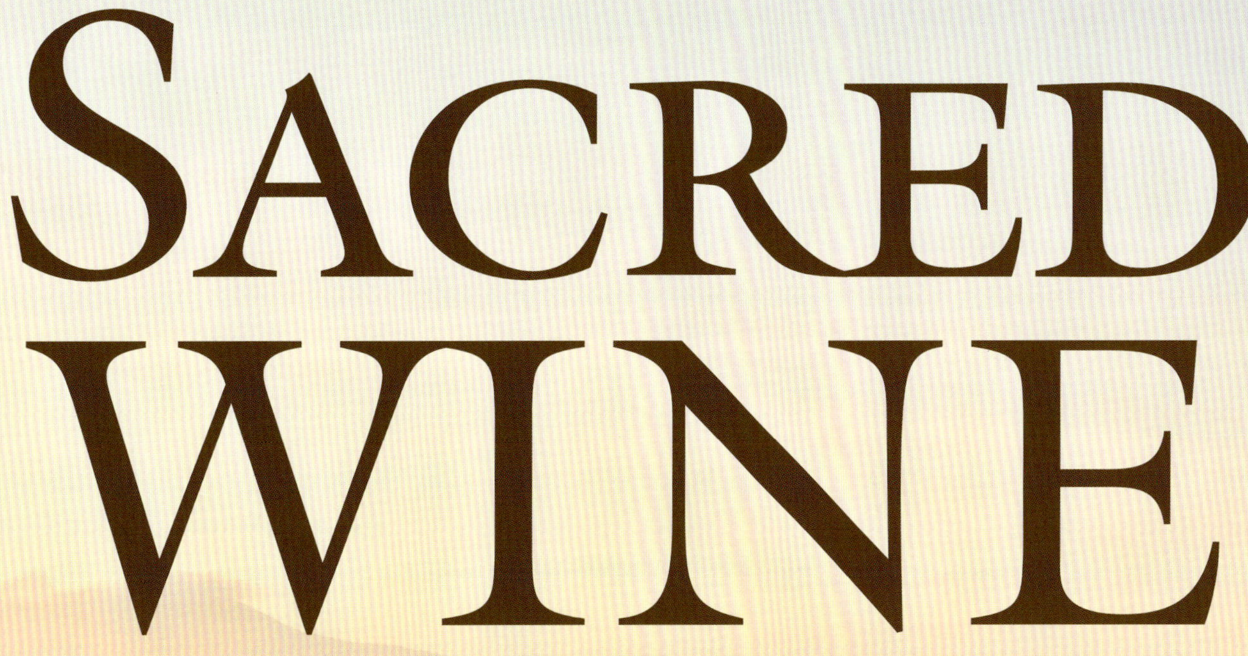

THE HOLY HISTORY AND HERITAGE OF CATHOLIC VINTNERS

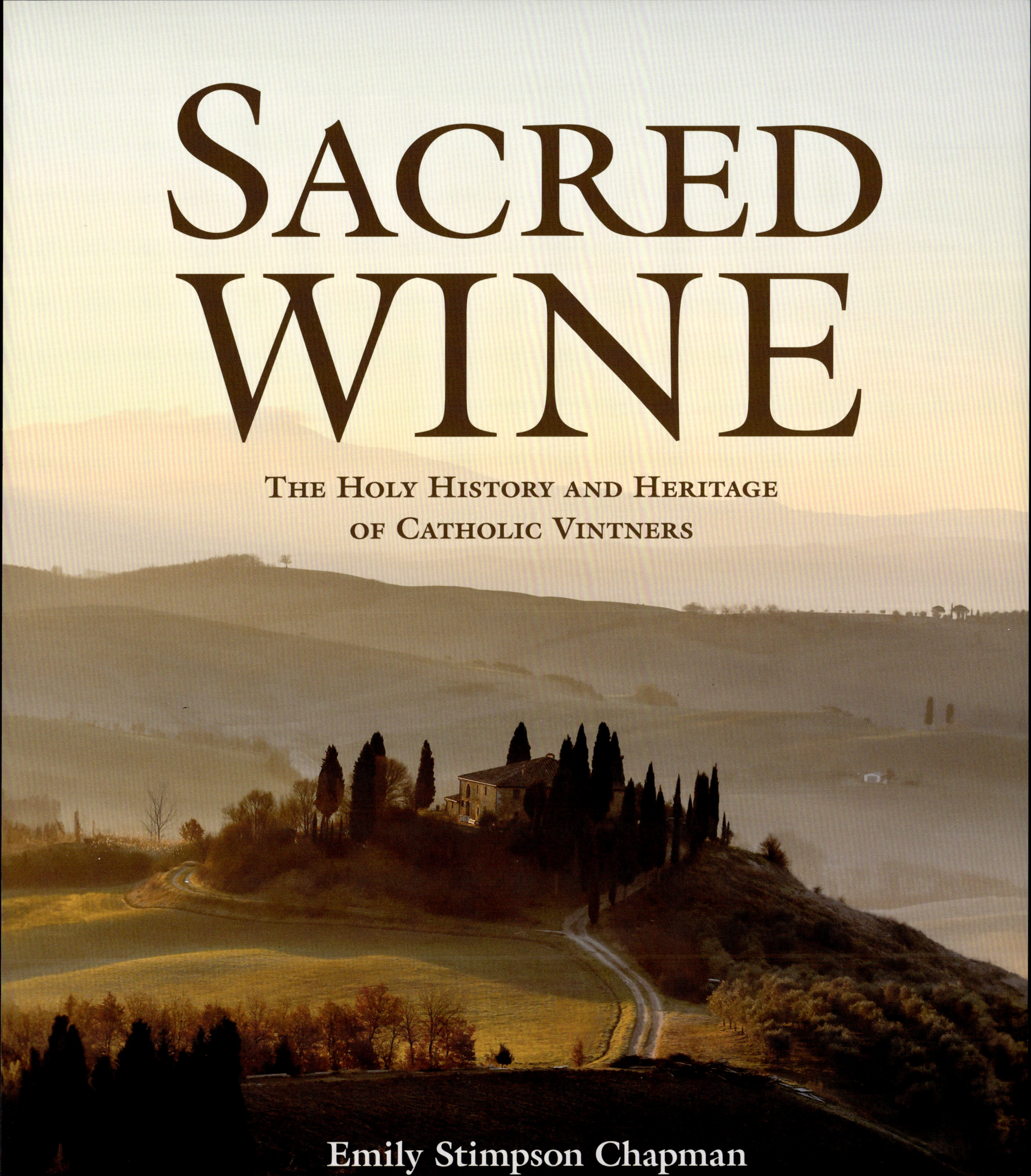

Emily Stimpson Chapman

Available from:
Marian Helpers Center
Stockbridge, MA 01263

Prayerline: 1-800-804-3823
Orderline: 1-800-462-7426
ShopMercy.org

Websites:
Marian.org
TheDivineMercy.org
DivineMercyPlus.org

Library of Congress Control Number: 2024945133
ISBN: 978-1-59614-631-0

Imprimi Potest:
Very Rev. Chris Alar, MIC
Provincial Superior, Blessed Virgin Mary, Mother of Mercy Province
Marian Fathers of the Immaculate Conception of the B.V.M.
July 11, 2025
Feast of St. Benedict of Nursia, Abbot

Nihil Obstat:
Robert A. Stackpole, STD
Censor Deputatus
July 11, 2025

Note: The *Nihil Obstat* and corresponding *Imprimi Potest* are not a certification that those granting it agree with the contents, opinions, or statements expressed in the work. Instead, they merely confirm that the work contains nothing contrary to faith and morals.

Copy Editing and Research: Rachel Salvetti

Editor: Mary Clark

Layout and Cover Design: Curtis Bohner

Brief portions of the chapters on Maison Drappier and Domaine Laroche began as part of a story on wine and saints for the Franciscan University of Steubenville's Alumni Magazine, Franciscan Way, Fall 2022.

"Wherever the Catholic sun doth shine,
There's always laughter and good red wine.
At least I've always found it so.
Benedicamus Domino!"

"The Catholic Sun," Hilaire Belloc

Table of Contents

Map of Europe 9

Introduction 11

- Italy
  - Castello di Magione 21
  - Abbazia di Monte Oliveto Maggiore 27
  - Abbazia di Novacella 35
- France
  - Abbaye de Lérins 41
  - Chateau Clos de Vougeot 47
  - Les Cordeliers 53
  - Maison Drappier 59
  - Abbaye Sainte-Madeleine du Barroux 65
  - Domaine Laroche 71
- Spain
  - Cellars De Scala Dei 79
  - Heras Cordón 87
  - The Royal Abbey of Santa Maria de Poblet 91

Photo Credits 98

Bibliography 99

About the Author 101

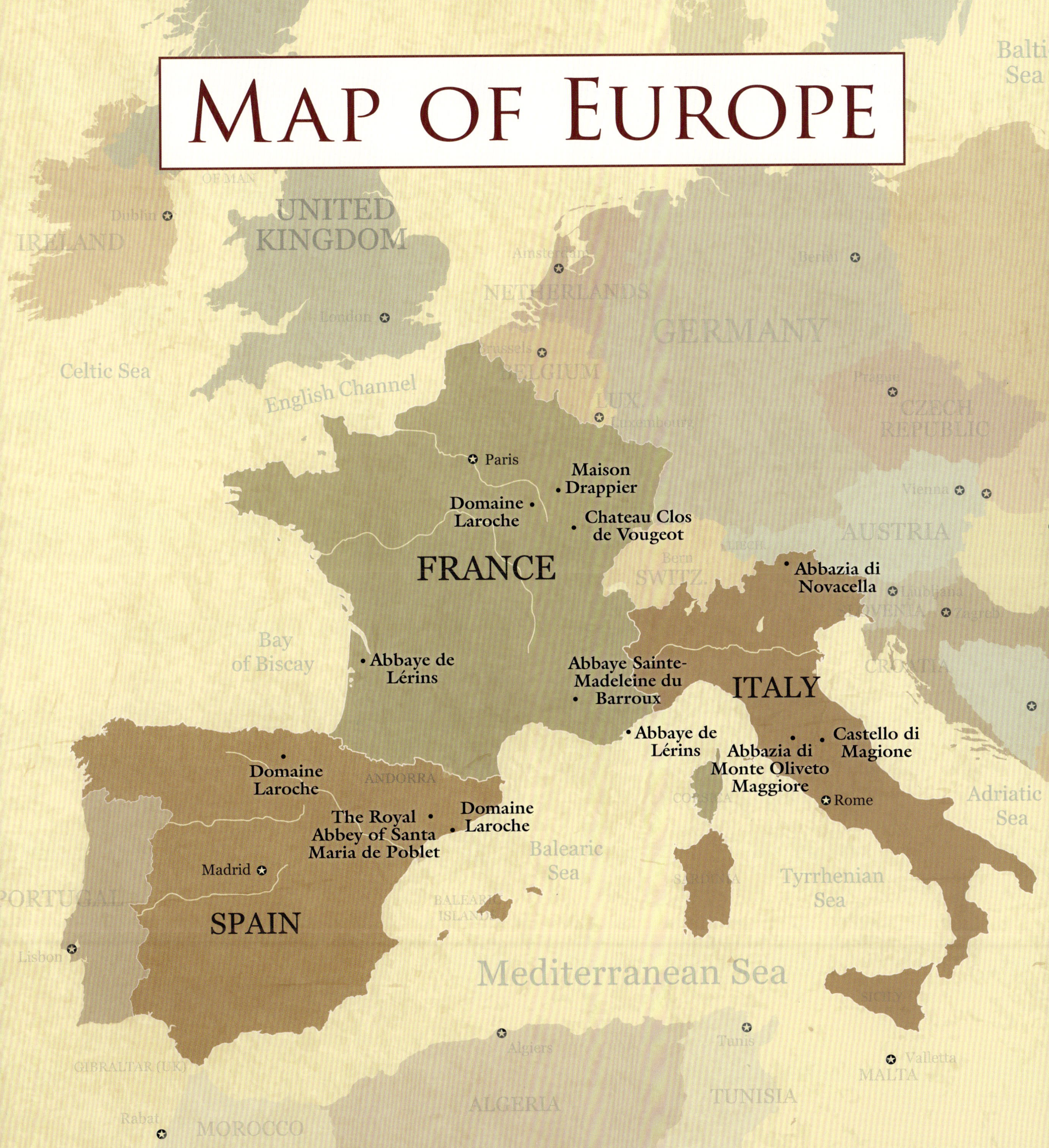
MAP OF EUROPE
UNITED KINGDOM
IRELAND
Dublin
London
Celtic Sea
English Channel
NETHERLANDS
Amsterdam
Brussels
BELGIUM
LUX.
GERMANY
Berlin
Prague
CZECH REPUBLIC
Vienna
AUSTRIA
Paris
Maison Drappier
Domaine Laroche
Chateau Clos de Vougeot
FRANCE
Bern
SWITZ.
Abbazia di Novacella
Bay of Biscay
Abbaye de Lérins
Abbaye Sainte-Madeleine du Barroux
ITALY
Abbaye de Lérins
Castello di Magione
Abbazia di Monte Oliveto Maggiore
Rome
CROATIA
Adriatic Sea
Domaine Laroche
ANDORRA
The Royal Abbey of Santa Maria de Poblet
Domaine Laroche
Madrid
SPAIN
PORTUGAL
Lisbon
Balearic Sea
Tyrrhenian Sea
Mediterranean Sea
Algiers
Tunis
Valletta
MALTA
GIBRALTAR (UK)
Rabat
MOROCCO
ALGERIA
TUNISIA
Baltic Sea

INTRODUCTION

"LIKE LIFE TO MAN": THE GIFT AND GLORY OF WINE

Every September, on a small island in the French Riviera, about a dozen Cistercian monks fan out across eight hectares of vineyards. In their traditional white and black habits, they work quickly, seeking to harvest the fruits of their year-long labor at the peak of perfection. In the weeks, months, and years to come, those fruits will be crushed and pressed, fermented, then clarified, aged, bottled, and eventually sold around the world.

The monks of the Abbaye de Lérins have been doing this work for at least 1,000 years. Some say the planting, picking, and making of wine has been the Abbey's business even longer, perhaps as far back as the late fourth century, when the hermit Saint Honorat made his home on the island that now bears his name.

Today, Saint-Honorat Island is one of only a handful of places in the world where you can find monks tending the vines. But long ago, in the centuries before reformation and revolution came to Europe, there would have been nothing remarkable about Cistercian monks making wine. There would have been nothing remarkable about any monks of any order making wine. For over a thousand years, throughout all of Christendom, tens of thousands of monks divided their days between chapel and vineyard, producing wines not only for their own consumption, but also for kings and queens, lords and ladies, and ordinary men and women from London to Prague.

That all changed when the Enlightenment swept across Europe, gradually convincing crowned heads and governments to dissolve the monasteries and send the religious who called them home out into the world. The vineyards once tended by monks and nuns passed into private hands, and the millennia-old connection between the Catholic faith and the sacred art of wine making was, in many places, all but forgotten.

Still, traces of that history remain. They linger in the Catholic names which adorn some of the world's finest bottles, in the ancient buildings which now house new presses and cellars, and in the wines themselves, which wouldn't exist without the dedication, innovation, and hard work of Catholic men and women who have long since departed this world to drink deeply in the heavenly banquet of the next.

A Sign of Blessing

Long before European religious orders turned grapes into wine, and even before Jesus transformed wine into His blood, the fruit of the vine was almost always more than a drink. It was a witness to the God Who created it, affirming both God's existence and God's goodness. Saint Paul, speaking to the people of Lystra, tells us this in the Book of Acts, saying, "In past generations [God] allowed all the nations to walk in their own ways; yet he did not leave himself without witness, for he did good and gave you from heaven rains and fruitful seasons, satisfying your hearts with food and gladness" (Acts 14:16-17).

There, Saint Paul is echoing the Psalmist, who proclaimed that wine is a gift from God, whose purpose is to "gladden the heart of man" (Ps 104:15).

In a world with no Eucharist, no images of God as a human baby resting in a cradle or as a grown man hanging from a cross, no Gospel of John telling us that "God so loved the world that He gave His only Son," and no saints radiating the Father's heart through the witness of their words and lives, there still was wine.

Like mountains that bore witness to God's majesty and oceans that witnessed to His power, wine bore witness to God's love. It spoke of a God who wanted His children to know joy, laughter, and peace. It proclaimed, by its very existence, that the God of the world was a good God who would provide the very best for His people, a superabundance of blessing — more love, more life, more grace than they imagined possible.

In all that, wine was a natural sign of a supernatural reality. It bore the mark of its Creator, proclaiming a fundamental truth about Him to help people know Him, love Him, and desire Him.

The ancient Israelites recognized this, and again and again in the Old Testament the patriarchs, prophets, and psalmists associate wine with God's blessing.

When Melchizedek, the King of Salem, (literally "King of Peace") blesses Abraham, he offers up both bread and wine. When Isaac hands on the family blessing to his son Jacob, his prayers include a petition for an abundance of grain and wine (Gen 27:28). In the Book of Numbers, God blesses the Levites by bestowing upon them the rights to Israel's best wine (Num 18:12). Later, in Deuteronomy, God promises Israel that if they obey Him, He will bless them in any number of ways, including with wine:

> And because you hearken to these ordinances, and keep and do them, the Lord your God will keep with you the covenant and the steadfast love which he swore to your fathers to keep; he will love you, bless you, and multiply you; he will also bless the fruit of your body and the fruit of your ground, your grain and your wine and your oil, the increase of your cattle and the young of your flock, in the land which he swore to your fathers to give you (Dt 7:12-13).

The Promised Land itself is described by Moses as a "land of grain and wine" (Dt 33:28). And when David finally ascends to the throne of Israel, the men who helped put him there, described in 1 Chronicles as "the army of God," celebrate that blessing with abundant wine (1 Chr 12:39-40).

Just as ample and good wine is recognized in the Old Testament as a sign of God's blessing, the lack of wine, like a lack of food, is seen as a curse. In Deuteronomy, Moses warns God's people that while obedience to God's covenant will result in good wine, disobedience will have an entirely different result. "You shall plant vineyards and dress them," he says, "but you shall neither drink of the wine nor gather the grapes, for the worm shall eat them" (Dt 28:39). He later elaborates on what disobedience will mean for the people:

> The Lord will bring a nation against you from afar, from the end of the earth, as swift as the eagle flies, a nation whose language you do not understand, a nation of stern countenance, who shall not regard the person of

the old or show favor to the young, and shall eat the offspring of your cattle and the fruit of your ground, until you are destroyed; who also shall not leave you grain, wine, or oil, the increase of your cattle or the young of your flock, until they have caused you to perish (Dt 28:49-51).

Too much wine is, of course, recognized as a problem in both the Old and New Testaments, with prophets like Isaiah and apostles like Paul condemning drunkenness (Is 5:11, Eph 5:18, Titus 2:3). Overwhelmingly, though, positive references to wine outnumber negative references, with 145 mentions of wine occurring in the context of blessing and worship and only 40 mentions appearing in the context of drunkenness and abuse.

From Sign to Reality

In the Old Testament, wine is a natural symbol of God's goodness and God's blessing. It doesn't lose that significance in the New Testament. It still symbolizes the superabundance of God's grace in the world. Jesus' first public miracle is to transform ordinary water for feet washing into the finest and most abundant of wines at Cana, signifying His power, goodness, and blessing (Jn 2:3-10).

Jesus also uses wine to symbolize the superabundance of grace in the Christian soul and how a new law, written on men's hearts, will supersede the ritual laws of the Pharisees: "And no one puts new wine into old wineskins; if he does, the new wine will burst the skins, and it will be spilled, and the skins will be destroyed. But new wine must be put into fresh wineskins" (Lk 5:37-38).

What changes in the New Testament is that wine becomes something far more than a sign of God's blessing. It becomes blessing. It becomes grace. It becomes Blood. It becomes Jesus Himself, with every drop of wine transfigured in the Liturgy of the New Covenant — the Holy Mass — containing a fullness of the Lord's Body, Blood, Soul, and Divinity.

This happened for the first time at the Last Supper. The night before Jesus died, as He gathered in the Upper Room with the twelve Apostles, He gave His disciples a new way to remember Him.

> And he took bread, and when He had given thanks, he broke it and gave it to them, saying, "This is my body which is given for you. Do this in remembrance of me." And likewise the cup after supper, saying, "This cup which is poured out for you is the new covenant in my blood" (Lk 22:19-20).

In the original Greek, the word translated here as "remembrance" is *anamnesis*, which literally means "to make the past present." This is what happens at every Catholic Mass, at every church in the world, when a priest repeats those words over bread and wine. The past becomes present. Bread becomes Body. Wine becomes Blood. Body and Blood become, as Jesus said they would, "real food" and "real drink," given to those who are reborn of water and Spirit. The sacrifice begun in the Upper Room and completed on the Cross is made present to ordinary believers in ordinary parishes on an ordinary day.

Or, perhaps it more deeply captures the truth of the mystery to say that when a priest prays those words in the Mass, the veil is drawn back between Heaven and earth, allowing ordinary believers in ordinary parishes on an ordinary day to worship with the angels and saints as the Great High Priest offers Himself once for all and gives Himself to all and allows all to feed on Him.

In the Mass, the events of the Last Supper and Good Friday are made present to us. And the now risen and glorified Body which sat at the table with the Apostles and hung on the Cross at Calvary is given to us. So too is the Blood that flowed from Christ's hands and feet when He was nailed to the Cross and that poured forth from His side when pierced by a lance. In the Eucharist, under the guise of bread and wine, Christ gives Himself to His people, filling us with His own divine life, sanctifying grace.

Through all eternity, God saw how salvation history would unfold. He knew every choice made by every man and every consequence that would follow from those choices. God has never been surprised by His creatures. He has never scrambled to figure out a Plan B because we upended His Plan A. Rather, like the universe's greatest chess player, He has foreseen our every move and gone before us and ahead of us to use those moves in ways we can't always imagine, with His every action in history and our lives designed to help guide us to the best possible end: Him.

As part of that cosmic orchestration, God wrote the world in a way similar to how we write books. He fashioned material objects and events to help us grasp immaterial realities. He created real people, real things, and real events that pointed to spiritual truths.

In other words, God, as the author of all things, created and directed human lives, events, and elements within creation to point beyond themselves, to become prefigurements of saving realities and help us understand supernatural truths. This is true of water and fire, doves and oil, the anointing of kings and the plights of the prophets. The waters of the flood point the way to the waters of Baptism. The flames which burn the bush without consuming it prefigure the tongues of fire of Pentecost. The wine poured out as blessing becomes blessing at the Last Supper, on Good Friday, and every day in the Holy Mass.

In God's perfect design, wine was always meant to be an ordinary sign that would point beyond itself to the extraordinary reality of the Eucharist. It was always meant to be a natural symbol of the very greatest supernatural truths. It was always meant to help us understand what is happening when a priest stands before us, raises up a cup, and proclaims the words: "Behold the Lamb of God."

This is why something of the sacred lingers about every grape and every glass. There's the potential for holiness in wine, a hint of something more to come, of some greater possibility, of some future transformation imaginable only through the sheer gratuitous gift of God.

This grace nourishes the life of God within us. It helps us to grow in faith and strengthens us in virtue. It heals us of venial sin. It comforts us in our sorrow, fills us with joy, and builds community within the Body of Christ. It gladdens the whole person — body, mind, heart, soul. It blesses the whole person — body, mind, heart, soul. It does on a supernatural level what wine has always done on a natural level, filling us not just with a sign of God's goodness and blessing, but filling us with the One who is Goodness and Blessing. The sign becomes the thing signified. The symbol becomes reality.

Wine's ability to do this, to become this, is not a coincidence. It's not happenstance. It's by design. It's how God intended it to be from the very beginning.

In that sense, wine is a bit like us — made for more, longing to be transformed, waiting for grace to do what grace does, pressed hard by life and its sorrows, maturing in quiet and hidden places, changing with age, seeking perfection, destined for glory.

A Catholic Tradition

That hint of the sacred, the promise of something more, the knowledge of what wine was made for — all that has informed the life of the Catholic Church from the first to the last.

Unlike our Protestant brothers and sisters, many of whom reject the goodness of wine because of its potential for abuse, Catholics see wine as a gift to treasure, not an evil to fear.

Yes, of course, wine can be misused and abused. For all of us, wine, if drunk past what Saint Thomas Aquinas called "the point of hilarity," becomes an occasion of sin and confessable matter. For some — the young, the sick, the addiction-inclined — even a mere sip is too much. But none of that makes wine itself bad. It's us — fallen, weak creatures, prone to sickness and death — that are the problem, not the wine. Nothing that God preordained from the dawn of creation to play such a pivotal role in our sanctification can be anything other than good. Especially a fine Bordeaux.

Over the past two millennia, the need for wine, not merely to drink, but to be offered up in the Mass, led monks and nuns across Europe and around the world to plant vineyards as soon as they finished building their monastery's walls … and sometimes even before that.

When Rome was still an empire, men and women dedicated to God grew grapes to make their own wine. After Rome collapsed and barbarian tribes destroyed cities and devastated land, more men and women dedicated to God built new monasteries and planted new vineyards. In those monasteries, they offered shelter and safety to local peasants, and, with those peasants, monks, brothers, and nuns replanted ancient vineyards that had gone fallow due to earlier invasions.

Those monks and nuns did more than that though. They made notes. They shared tips and tricks with other houses from their order. As they grew old, they passed down what they learned to the younger religious who took their place working the land and pressing the wine. They experimented, trying different grapes in different plots of land and different soils. They took advantage of one of the greatest gifts religious life gave them: time, using it to carefully study and perfect every step of the winemaking process, from cultivating seedlings to bottling the work of their hands.

The result was a revolution in winemaking. *Clos Vougeot*, Chablis, Champagne, *Chenin Blanc* — some of the greatest wines ever made and some of the most significant advances in winemaking, from corks to oaken barrels, owe their origins to Catholic monks and nuns of centuries past.

Even here, in the Americas, this holds true. The first vineyards established in the New World were often planted by priests and brothers who sailed from Spain to evangelize the Americas. This is especially true in California, where Saint Junipero Serra laid the

groundwork for the future state's magnificent wine industry, planting the first vineyards and building its first wineries up and down the coast. Wherever Serra established a mission — Los Angeles, San Diego, Santa Clara, San Francisco, Sonoma, and more — he also established a vineyard. Serra, in turn, relied upon methods developed by the missionaries he worked with in Mexico and planted a varietal that the Franciscan friars there had cultivated. America's wine industry began with a varietal still called "The Mission Grape."

In the end, try as we might, there is no untangling the history of the Church and the history of wine. The two have been bound up together since the first grapes burst forth on the first vines, which was perhaps in Eden under the watchful eyes of Adam and Eve.

The Church and wine also will continue to be bound up together, right up to the Last Day, when all who have called upon Christ's name and become adopted sons and daughters of God in Baptism, will sit down at the Marriage Supper of the Lamb, where, as Isaiah prophesied:

> On this mountain the Lord of hosts will make for all peoples a feast of fat things, a feast of wine on the lees, of fat things full of marrow, of wine on the lees well refined. And he will destroy on this mountain the covering that is cast over all peoples, the veil that is spread over all nations. He will swallow up death for ever, and the Lord God will wipe away tears from all faces, and the reproach of his people he will take away from all the earth; for the Lord has spoken (Is 25:6-8).

Just as there is no untangling the history of the Church and the history of wine, there also is no telling a complete history of Catholicism and wine, at least not in one book. Thousands of monasteries over thousands of years have been a part of that history. Whole libraries could be dedicated to telling the stories of faithful men and women and the grapes they grew.

That is, libraries could be dedicated to those stories if so many of them hadn't been lost. Wherever religious orders have been suppressed and monasteries dissolved, buildings have crumbled, records have been destroyed, and important history forgotten.

Nevertheless, there is still some of that story to tell. There is also some of that story still being written, as the old traditions live on or are resurrected in out-of-the way abbeys in Italy, France, Germany, and elsewhere.

Tasting Stories

The book you're holding in your hand tells 12 of those stories, featuring 12 wineries whose existences have been shaped by the Catholic faith. Most of the wineries began as monasteries. A few still are monasteries. But in each, the history first written by the Benedictines, Cistercians, Carthusians, Franciscans, and more, lives on.

Some of the wines produced in these wineries can be bought here in the United States. Most (but not all) of the rest can be shipped here. It's good to drink these wines and know you're drinking part of the Church's history and (in some cases) even supporting that history as it continues to unfold.

It's better though, if possible, to drink the wines in the places where they were made, to walk the land where the grapes were grown, hear the stories told about them in the cellars where the bottles age, and pray in the churches where the men and women who first grew the grapes once prayed … or still do pray.

I hope this book will help you to do both. It aims to give you the stories behind the wineries through introductions to the orders or saints that established them, pictures of the rules of life that informed their work, and accounts of the secular history which shaped the wineries' history, as well as introduce you to a few of the wines being made in each winery today. Also, as much as possible, it will provide you with some of the information necessary to visit the wineries, taste their wine, and buy a bottle or two.

Whether you ever manage to taste the bottles written about here or only sip close approximations purchased in your local wine store, this book will help you taste it all with joy and prayer, appreciating more deeply the men and women whose faith helped put that glass in your hand and recognizing that each sip of wine is a gift, "like life to man," meant to bring "rejoicing of heart and gladness of soul" (Sir 31:27-28).

It also will help you remember what, by God's grace, every drop of wine has the potential to become: Life itself, the Blood of the One who is "the Way, the Truth, and the Life."

Last of all, with each glass you pour and each wine of which you drink deeply, may you never forget that the wine you behold with your eyes, smell with your nose, and taste on your tongue also bears witness to the work Christ is doing in you. He is caring for you, cultivating you, transforming you, maturing you. He is making you not just good or fine, but holy, sacred. Day by day, year by year, in ways often too imperceptible for you to see but that will be evident to all at the end of time, He is making you His own.

ITALY

ITALIE
DALMATI
Ravenna
Roma
Napoli
Sicile
Catania
Saragusa
Ortona
Pescara
Ancona
Manfredonia
Bari
Palermo
Trapano
Messina
Ustica
Stromboli
Lipari
Pantelaria
C. Passero
C. delle Colonne
Ragusa
Spolato
I. Tremiti
I. Ponza
Ischia
Valona
Primero
Piombino

The Via Francigena in Italy today,
a well traveled pilgrimage route once more.

Castello di Magione

Magione, Italy

Without Pope Urban II, the Perugian winery Sagravit would not exist. Or, at the very least, its home, Castello di Magione, would not exist.

The story of Castello di Magione begins in 1095, when Urban traveled to France to give an important address to French noblemen. At the time, Islam was once again on the march, and Urban was determined to stop it.

A Protracted Battle

Five centuries earlier, adherents to Islam were few, and Christianity was the faith of an empire. In 632, the year of the death of Mohammad, the founder of Islam, Palestine, Syria, Egypt, Asia Minor, and all of North Africa, as well as Spain, France, Italy, and the islands of Sicily, Sardinia, and Corsica were considered Christian lands. Then, Islam's push north, east, and west began. A century later, Palestine, Egypt, Syria, North Africa, Spain, Southern France, and most of Asia Minor had all fallen to invading Muslim armies and were Christian no more.

Over the next 250 years, Islam's push north continued, with Arab forces invading Italy in the ninth century and sacking Old St. Peter's Basilica in Rome, in 846. The Christian rulers of both East and West pushed back, but the protracted battle they waged was almost always defensive, and their only victories were in France, Italy, and portions of Spain. The rest of the conquered territories, including the Holy Land, remained under Muslim control.

Throughout the long, bloody conflict there had been one saving grace. The Arab Muslims who controlled Palestine had almost always shown great respect for both the Christian holy sites and the pilgrims who traveled to pray there.

In the mid-11th century, however, the Turks, who had only recently converted to Islam, invaded the Holy Land, conquering their Arab brothers. The Turks looked less kindly on the Christian holy sites than the Arabs did, and, in short order, turned the ancient churches into mosques. They also made it clear to Christian pilgrims that their presence was no longer welcome.

After their victory in the Holy Land was complete, the Turks set their sights on the Byzantine Empire. Recognizing that his troops were no match for the Turkish armies, the Holy Roman Emperor Alexius begged for help from the West. The first person he begged, Pope Gregory VII, was sympathetic but too preoccupied with his own problems to do anything. Fortunately for Alexius, Gregory's papacy was short-lived (a mere two years), and his successor, Urban II, was eager to help Byzantium out.

This brings us back to Claremont, and Urban's words to the French nobleman. The time had come, the pope told them, to push back against the Islamic aggressors, not just by resisting them at home, but by taking the battle to them and reclaiming the lands which had first professed their faith in Christ. Urban called upon nobles and peasants alike to rise up, travel to the Holy Land, and defeat the Turkish invaders.

There were some false starts and stumbles, but in the end, Christian Europe heeded Urban's call, and, in 1099, Christian forces reclaimed the Holy Land, where they established the four Latin "kingdoms": Edessa, Antioch, Tripoli, and Jerusalem.

For 45 years, the Holy Land remained in Christian hands. Then, in 1144, Muslims retook Edessa, and Saint Bernard of Clairvaux took it upon himself to call for a Second Crusade.

It was after this call that Castello di Magione was built.

A Knightly Order

A century earlier, under the leadership of Blessed Fra Gerard, a group of Amalfi Christians working in the Holy Land had committed themselves to caring for pilgrims there. They formed a religious community and opened a hostel that welcomed all people of good will who needed food, a bed, or just a place to rest. Their job became more difficult with the coming of the Turks in 1071, so, in addition to providing shelter, they took on the role of bodyguards for those willing to risk a journey to Jesus' native land. With the advent of the Crusades, their protective mission morphed into a military one, and they were formally recognized by the pope in 1113 as the Knights Hospitaller.

In the years that followed, many Knights remained in the Holy Land, defending Christians from attack and helping lead the military efforts to defend (and later reestablish) the four Latin kingdoms.

Other Knights, however, went west and began building hostels along the most frequently-traveled roads to the Holy Land. One of these hostels was the Castello di Magione. It was constructed around 1150 in Umbria, along the Francigena Road, which started in Canterbury, England, continued through Rome, and ended in Jerusalem.

The Knights who built the hostel first constructed a large Romanesque chapel, dedicated to Saint John the Baptist. They also built a dormitory and refectory, where guests could eat and sleep. Later, as the order took on more military functions, the simple original structures were added on to or replaced by the stone castle that stands today.

In the centuries that followed, as the Crusades waxed and waned and all four kingdoms were eventually lost, the Castle became a common meeting place for popes, kings, and nobles. Unfortunately, not all that transpired within its walls was holy business. It was there that the conspiracy against Cesare Borgia, made infamous in Machiavelli's political classic *The Prince*, was conceived.

Eventually, the Knights Hospitaller left the Holy Land altogether, settling first in Rhodes (in modern day Greece) and later on the island of Malta. As their locations changed, so did their name, and now they are known formally as The Sovereign Military Hospitaller Order of Saint John of Jerusalem of Rhodes and of Malta. More commonly, they're referred to as the Knights of Malta. Not since the days of Napoleon, however, have they had any military function. Instead, the Knights have gone back to their charitable roots and today sponsor medical missions in more than 120 countries. Their members, who increasingly come from the United States, are laymen and women who take a vow of obedience to the pope. And the only building they call their own is their headquarters in Rome.

Preserving Traditions

Although the Knights have been gone from the Castello di Magione for centuries, their legacy lives on there, both in the hospitality offered to visitors and in the wine served to those visitors.

It was the Knights who, back in the 12th century, planted the Castle's first vineyards in the hills surrounding Lake Trasimeno and first turned the grapes into wine for weary pilgrims. Today, those vineyards are managed by the *Societá Agricola Vitivinicola Italiana* (Sagravit), which ensures that the ancient farming wisdom of Italy is safeguarded for future generations.

On the property's 530 hectares (32 under vine), Sagravit grows a wide range of grapes. Fifty-five percent are red, including Pinot Nero, Merlot, Gamay, Cabernet Sauvignon, Sangiovese, and Canaiolo. The remaining 45 percent are white, primarily Grechetto, as well as Chardonnay, Sauvignon Blanc, and Trebbiano.

In their new state-of-the-art winery, built in 2009, Sagravit produces 10 wines, including their premier *Novacento Rosso*. Made annually, it is dedicated to the anniversary of the signing of the papal bull in 1113 by Pope Paschal II, which formally recognized the Sovereign Military Order of Malta and placed it under the direct protection of the Holy See. A complex red, made up of 85 percent Merlot grapes and 15 percent Sangiovese, *Novacento* has notes of cinnamon, fruit, chocolate, and black pepper. It pairs well with pasta Bolognese, roasted veal, and dark chocolate.

Other notable wines include their rosé, the *Belfiore*, made from Gamay, a cultivar dating back to the 15th century. Fruit-forward

and complex, with delicate floral aromas, *Belfiore* is best enjoyed with a light appetizer such as melon and prosciutto, salad Niçoise, or a potato and leek quiche.

The *Nerocavalieri*, which was made in tribute to the Knights of Malta from 100 percent Pinot Noir grapes, is also excellent. Ruby red with purple highlights, this well-balanced wine has a delicate bouquet and a slight sweetness on the palate. It tastes its best when served with salty, savory dishes, such as bacon and sage risotto or roasted pork loin with garlic and rosemary, as well as with chocolate-covered strawberries.

Visiting Castello di Magione

Wine tastings are by reservation only. Visitors can choose from four different wine tasting experiences. The Castle's wine shop is located in the beautiful cloister.

For more information:
E-mail: info@terredeicavalieri.it
Telephone: +39 075 5057319
Website: www.CastellodiMagione.it/en/

Abbazia di
Monte Oliveto
Maggiore
1319
Toscana
Indicazione Geografica
A.D. 2019

Abbazia di Monte Oliveto Maggiore

Asciano, Italy

Forty-five minutes from Siena, in the grey hills of Tuscany, stands the Abbey of Monte Oliveto Maggiore. There, a community of Benedictine monks live, pray, practice hospitality, and make wine, all in accordance with the Benedictine rule.

That rule, which gave rise to more than a millennium of labor in the vineyards for monks across Europe, reflects Saint Benedict of Nursia's desire to chart a way of life for religious that worked with and not against human nature.

Rule of Life

Born around the year 480 to a noble Roman family in the city of Nursia, Benedict fled city life for solitude in the country when he was just 20 years old. In the years that followed, he lived as both hermit and abbot, founding monastic communities in Lazio, including (most notably) the Monte Cassino Abbey. He wrote his rule in the early sixth century, after watching the men he directed struggle — and often fail — in their attempts to live a life centered

on the Gospel. Through the years, Benedict had learned the hard way what did and didn't work for those striving to follow Christ in a singular way, and his rule attempted to put those lessons at the service of his monks.

The first lesson Benedict learned was that almost no one is cut out to be a hermit. Human beings, he understood, are made for communion — with God and others — and the Christian life is one best lived and realized in community.

Second, he learned that work is a necessary part of pursuing holiness. Although the Roman culture of Benedict's birth saw work as the province of slaves and leisure as the goal of life, Benedict took the opposite approach. He recognized, as the old saying goes, that idle hands are the devil's workshop and that honest labor serves as the foundation for moral growth. More fundamentally, in light of Christ's Passion, death, and Resurrection, he saw that the difficulties of work could be offered up to God and become salvific.

Finally, Benedict learned that prayer must be the heart of work and life, the source from which all other works take their inspiration, direction, and strength.

Benedict organized his Rule around those lessons.

In addition to requiring his monks to make the usual vows of poverty, chastity, and obedience, the Benedictine Rule also required monks to make a commitment to stability, promising to remain in one monastery for the whole of their religious life. This was intended to foster community life and help men avoid the "restless self-will" that Benedict believed all too often led monastic undertakings to fail.

The Rule also provided a strict schedule for the monks, ensuring that they kept busy with physical and intellectual labors, which would, in some way, benefit the life of the community, provide for the monks, and generate enough income or goods to care for the poor.

As for prayer, the Rule stipulated that when the monks weren't working they should be praying. Together, they prayed the

Psalms seven times a day, plus Night Prayer, and participated in the celebration of the Mass.

Lastly, the Rule required the monasteries to use their wealth to offer temporary shelter and food to guests, receiving everyone who came to them as they would receive Christ Himself.

A Different Vision

Well before the 13th century, the Benedictine Rule was far and away the most common monastic rule in the Roman Catholic world. Nevertheless, when Saint Bernardo Tolomei, the founder of the Abbey at Monte Oliveto Maggiore, was tasked with establishing a religious order, he thought he could improve upon the Rule, supplementing it with requirements of his own.

Tolomei was born in 1272 to a wealthy Sienese family. Legend has it that even as a boy, he longed to join the Dominicans, but his family forbade it. So he instead studied law, both civil and canon, taught philosophy at the University of Siena, and served in the city's government. Around 1312, however, Tolomei temporarily lost his sight. He turned to the Blessed Virgin Mary and begged her to restore his vision. When she did, he vowed to dedicate himself to religious life, regardless of his family's opinion.

Soon after, in 1313, Tolomei left Siena with two companions and retreated to his family's property in Accona. There, the three lived as hermits, embracing a life of penance, prayer, silence, and abstinence from wine or any strong drink. Five years later, after their asceticism raised eyebrows in Rome, Tolomei's bishop asked him to embrace instead the official rules for religious life, and establish a religious congregation. With the help of his companions, he began building the Abbey of Monte Oliveto Maggiore. The labor was intense, with the men even producing the bricks on their own from the clay of the region. When the abbey was complete, it became the first home of Tolomei's newly established religious order: the Congregation of the Blessed Virgin of Monte Oliveto (also known as the Olivetans).

National Geographic *named the Abbey of Monte Oliveto Maggiore one of the "25 Best Places in the World to Travel in 2025."*

The historic exposed brick cellars in the basement of the monastery date to the 14th century.

Over the next two decades, Tolomei would establish eight more monasteries in eight Italian cities. In every one of them, the strictest possible penitential practices of the Benedictine Rule were embraced. For example, although St. Benedict had allowed his monks to drink a small portion of wine each day, Tolomei preached a gospel of radical abstention. In every place where Tolomei established a monastery, he ordered that any existing wine presses be destroyed and the ancient vineyards be uprooted.

In 1348, while nursing the poor, Tolomei and the brethren of the monastery in Siena contracted the plague; Tolomei died soon after. Celebrated as a "martyr of charity," he was beatified in 1644 by Pope Innocent X. Not until 2009, however, during the papacy of Pope Benedict XVI, was he declared a saint.

Return to Tradition

Tolomei's practices proved difficult for many of his monks to abide by during his lifetime. After his death, it proved all but impossible, and the strict ascetic standards he established were soon abandoned in favor of St. Benedict's more reasonable prescriptions.

Today, the Abbey of Monte Oliveto Maggiore continues to serve as the Motherhouse for the Olivetan congregation, which also has monasteries in France, Italy, the United Kingdom, Ireland, Israel, Korea, Mexico, Guatemala, Brazil, and the United States (New Mexico). Except for the white habits that the Olivetan monks wear, the entire congregation follows the conventional Benedictine Rule.

In accordance with that rule, the monks live, pray, and work as brothers. Every weekday at 7:30 a.m. and at 11:00 a.m. on Sundays, they chant the Holy Mass, and throughout the day and night they pray the office of the Church together. To support the monastery, they work the land, and, from the fruits of their labors, make olive oil, cereals, liquors, and wine. They also welcome guests year-round to their retreat house and open their gates daily to those wishing to tour the monastery, pray with the monks, and sample their delicious wines.

Those visitors pray in the Abbey's grand Baroque chapel, admire the architecture of its ancient library and refectory, and stroll through the 15th century cloister walk. There, they can look upon 35 frescoes, which depict the life of Saint Benedict. Painted by the artists Luca Signorelli and Antonio Bazzi, the frescoes are considered masterpieces of the Italian renaissance and are alone worth the visit to the monastery.

The Superior General of the Marian Congregation, the Most Rev. Joseph Roesch, MIC, traveled to the Abbey and visited with Dom Benedetto Maria Vichi. Watch the video on ***DivineMercyPlus.org/SacredWine****.*

After touring the monastery, visitors are invited to make their way to the monastery's wine cellars, where they can sample and purchase the wines made there.

Currently, the monastery winery produces 10 wines, including one made exclusively for the Holy Mass. The grapes for their wines are grown on 39 acres surrounding the monastery. Situated about 1,000 feet above sea level, on yellow sand and clay soil, the vineyard's most thriving varietal is Sangiovese. A Tuscan specialty, it is considered a chameleon of a grape because of its ability to produce both fruit forward wines and more rustic bottles that can taste chocolatey or smoky.

The monks' premier red, the *Monaco Rosso*, is a dry IGT wine made from a blend of Cabernet Sauvignon, Sangiovese, and Merlot. Aged 12 months in French oak barrels (*tonneaux*), it eventually develops a mildly herbaceous scent. With initial hints of red fruit and oak, the *Monaco Rosso* has a smoky finish and medium tannins. It pairs well with cured meats like prosciutto and speck, mature Parmesan cheeses, mushroom risottos, or lamb stews.

The monks of Monte Oliveto also make a full-bodied *Toscana 1319*, likewise blended from Cabernet Sauvignon, Sangiovese, and Merlot, with earthy vegetable notes, a hint of truffle, and an oaky finish. Both more acidic and with stronger tannins than the *Rosso*, it is excellent when served with beef Wellington, chicken cacciatore, or pan-fried gnocchi with sage and butter.

Outstanding among the Abbey's other wines is a crisp, dry rosé, made from 100 percent Sangiovese grapes, with floral notes and a mild taste of grapefruit, as well as a white made from Vermentino grapes, which has strong notes of honey and lime. Both are the perfect complement to a light salad, such as tuna and white beans with boiled eggs, a shrimp cocktail, or a seafood pasta such as spaghetti allo scoglio.

Visiting Abbazia de Monte Oliveto Maggiore

The Abbey is open to visitors year-round. Admission is free. Catholic faithful who visit the monastery are invited to join the monks for Mass at 7:30 a.m. on weekdays and 11:00 a.m. on Sundays. All visitors are also welcome to dine in the on-site, independently-run restaurant, La Torre, which serves lunch and dinner.

For more information:
E-mail: abbazia@monteolivetomaggiore.it
Telephone: +39 0577 707258
Website: www.MonteOlivetoMaggiore.it

Abbazia di Novacella

Bressanone, Italy

In the northernmost corner of Italy, almost hidden in the Alps, an order of priests lives together in community, following a way of life first charted over 1,600 years ago by the legendary Bishop of Hippo: Saint Augustine. Together, they teach, care for the poor, and minister in parishes throughout the South Tyrol region. They also make wine.

The Rule of Saint Augustine

Sometime around the year 400, Saint Augustine of Hippo sat down and wrote out a rule for himself and the priests who lived with him in his episcopal residence. The Bishop of Hippo believed that while priests weren't called to live exactly like monks, their priestly vocations were best lived in community. After all, he reasoned, the human person was made for community — for communion with God and man — and priests were no exception.

The rules he laid out for his priestly housemates were simple. They would root their life in prayer and hold property in common. Charity would guide all their interactions with one another. Chastity would order their relationships with women. Temperance and fasting would order their relationship with food. And quick apologies and ready forgiveness would order their inclinations to pride and anger. Saint Augustine also stressed the importance of

The interior of the Abbey church was redesigned in the Baroque style around 1740.

his priests caring for the poor and tending to the sick in imitation of the great High Priest, Jesus Christ.

Throughout the fifth century, the Augustinian rule spread beyond North Africa to Italy, Spain, and elsewhere, giving shape to the community life of both monks and priests. By 492, it shaped even the life of the pope, with Pope Gelasius implementing it for the priests of the Basilica of St. John Lateran, where he lived and served.

As the Roman Empire continued to crumble, however, and both Church and culture suffered from invasion, plague, and corruption, the influence of Saint Augustine's rule faded. In the monasteries, it was Saint Benedict's Rule that guided daily life, while priests increasingly lived alone (or worse, with illicit wives and concubines).

Not until the rise of Hildebrand (the future Pope Gregory VII) and other great reformers in the mid-11th century, did Saint Augustine's rule make a comeback. At the Lateran Synod of 1059, Hildebrand championed the rule as an important component of reforming clerical life. The synod fathers and the pope agreed with him and officially endorsed it as a pathway to renewal.

While the rule was intended to govern the life of all the ordained, in time it gave rise to a new order of priests, dedicated to living out that rule: the Canons Regular of St. Augustine, more commonly known as the Augustinian Canons.

Throughout the Middle Ages, the Augustinian Canons helped the faith flourish in shrines, parishes, and university towns. Some of the leading churches and cathedrals of the day were put in their charge, including the Shrine of Our Lady of Walsingham in England, the cathedrals of Saint John Lateran in Rome and St. Andrews in Scotland, as well as the diocesan cathedrals in Salzburg, Toledo, Saragossa, and elsewhere. In many of the cities where they served, the Canons built hospitals to serve the poor and schools for boys.

Some of the priests ministered in parishes, living out Saint Augustine's concern for pastoral care. And everywhere the order established itself, great care was given to the sacred Liturgy, particularly to the singing of sacred music.

Like monastic religious orders, the Canons take vows of poverty, chastity, and obedience. Unlike those orders, however, which are comprised of both priests and lay brothers, the Canons are comprised almost exclusively of priests. This, Saint Thomas Aquinas explained, is because the priesthood is essential to the life of a Canon, not to the life of a monk. Similarly, the care of souls is also essential to the life of a Canon, whereas the care of his community and the souls of his brother monks are essential to the life of the monk.

The Canons Regular of South Tyrol

It was that concern for the souls in his diocese that, in 1133, lead the newly appointed bishop of Bressanone, an Augustinian Canon named Hartmann, to establish a new monastery just three miles from his cathedral. The monastery was to be made up entirely of Canons Regular and dedicate itself to the pastoral care of people in the surrounding villages. Named Novacella, the Abbey quickly attracted patrons from the local nobility and flourished, becoming the spiritual and cultural heart of the South Tyrol region.

Although a fire in 1190 destroyed all the original buildings, the Canons quickly rebuilt and then continued adding on to the monastery throughout the late Middle Ages and Renaissance. Today, visitors can still see the fruit of that work, from the late Gothic choir with its characteristic steep roof, to its magnificent Gothic altar panels created by the renowned artists of the day (especially Michael and Friedrich Pacher, the Meister von Uttenheim, and Max Reichlich), as well as the Abbey's *scriptorium*, which houses hundreds of richly adorned manuscripts.

The continued existence of these treasures, however, is something of a miracle, given the continual abuse the Abbey suffered at the hands of warring powers.

Situated in Bressanone (or Brixen, in German), the Abbey sits just south of Austria, in what was, for millennia, the most important trade route across the Alps. Throughout its long history, which dates to at least 15 B.C., Bressanone was alternately controlled by Germanic powers (most frequently Bavaria), the Holy Roman Empire, and, later, by Austria and the Austro-Hungarian Empire. Only at the end of World War I, when Italy seized South Tyrol, did it officially become part of the Italian state.

Before then, the monastery endured every sort of indignity. It was plundered by Protestant peasants in the first decades of the Reformation, occupied by both German and French troops during the Napoleonic Wars, temporarily dissolved by the secularizing Bavarian government in 1807 (and subsequently stripped of many of its treasures), occupied by troops again in World War I, seized by Nazis and used as a warehouse and printshop in World War II, then bombed by the Allies in the same war.

In the end, however, Novacella not only survived; it thrived.

Today, 18 Canons Regular and two clerics live at the Novacella monastery. Together, they oversee the pastoral care of 18 parishes, a boarding school, and an educational center. Also, as their predecessors have done before them for almost 900 years, they administer a successful wine estate.

An Alpine Winery

Established in 1142, the Abbazia di Novacella winery is one of the oldest active wineries in the world. The Canons began planting vines on their land almost immediately after arriving in Bressanone, and every time they acquired new land in the area surrounding the monastery, they planted more vines. Due to the dissolution of the monastery in 1807, however, none of the terraced vineyards that immediately surround the Abbey are now owned by the Canons. Instead, the local farmers grow the grapes and bring them to the Abbey, which then takes over the winemaking process.

Those grapes are almost all white, and include varietals such as Sylvaner, Müller-Thurgau, Kerner, and Riesling. Due to the Alpine climate, the Canons plant them in areas with strong southern exposure, each variety precisely matched to a micro-location in which it can thrive.

Farther south, in vineyards actually owned by the Abbey, the red varietals of Schiava, Pinot Nero, and the sweet Moscato Rosa grow.

From these grapes, the Abbey produces two lines of wine: the Classic selection, which contains 13 fresh, fruity wines (nine white, four red), which are meant to be enjoyed young, and the Praepositus selection of exceptional, award-winning cru wines, (eight white, two red, two dessert) which can be aged for 10 years or longer.

Among the Praepositus selection, particular standouts are the *Grüner Veltliner* — a dry, golden white (similar to *Sauvignon Blanc*, but heartier), with early hints of ripe apples, quince, and honey on the palate, and a finish that recalls anise and pepper — and the Pinot Nero *Riserva*. The *Riserva* is ruby-red and velvety structured, with an initial earthy scent before swirling the glass and fragrances of cinnamon and cloves after swirling. On the palate, there is a subtle taste of cherries and wild raspberries.

Despite its Austrian origins, the *Gruner Veltliner* pairs beautifully with spicy Indian and Asian dishes, like palak paneer or a Vietnamese noodle salad. The Pinot Nero is exceptional with sausage and mushroom risotto, as well as with smoked salmon or roasted chicken.

Of the two dessert wines, the *Moscato Rosa* stands out. Fragrant with rose, fig, bitter chocolate, and coffee, it tastes of cherries and walnuts with a raspberry finish. Sweet without being jammy, it can be enjoyed with desserts like brie and fruit, vanilla gelato, or a spiced biscotti.

Visiting Novacella Abbey

Novacella Abbey is open Monday through Saturday. Guided Abbey tours and guided vineyard tours are offered. Reservations are required.

The museum and garden can be visited without a guide. Visitors are also welcome to dine at the Abbey Pub (Stiftskeller), housed in the Abbey's former mill.

For more information:
E-mail: info@kloster-neustift.it
Telephone: +39 0472 836 189
Website: www.Kloster-Neustift.it/en/

FRANCE
ANGLETERRE
PAYS BAS
LUXEMBOURG
LA MANCHE
OCÉAN
ESPAGNE
MER MÉDITE
GOLFE DE LYON
Monts Pyrennées
CARTE
DE LA FRANCE
DIVISÉE
EN SES 83. DÉPARTEMENS
Verifiée
Au Comité de Constitution
Sur les Originaux des Plans
de chaque Département
Presentée dans un Ordre Méthodique et
DÉDIÉE
A L'ASSEMBLÉE NATIONALE
Par les Auteurs de l'Atlas
National de France.
En 1790.
Lieues de 2280 Toises ou de 25 au Degré.
1 2 3 4 5 10 15 20 25
Explication des Signes
Chef lieu de Département et de District.
Chef lieu de la 1.ere Assemblée pour déliberer.
Chef lieu de District.
Lieu devant partager les Etablissements du District.
Réclamation non portée aux Décrets.

Abbaye de Lérins

Isle de Honoratus, France

Every May, the wealthy, powerful, and famous gather in the Mediterranean resort town of Cannes to watch some of the year's most important films and indulge in everything luxurious the world has to offer. More than a handful of those visitors, however, will leave luxury behind for a day and catch a boat to a small island less than four miles off the coast whose only residents are a group of monks. Some of the island's visitors are attracted by the chance to pray with the monks. Most, however, are attracted by the wines made by the monks.

A Place Apart

The story of the island's connection to the monks begins in 350 A.D., in what is now modern-day France but was then called Gaul. That year, a wealthy Roman couple gave birth to a son, Honoratus.

Over the next two decades, Honoratus received an excellent education, with the expectation that he would follow in his father's footsteps and become a government official. He then went and dashed those expectations at the age of 18, when, along with his brother Venantius, Honoratus converted to Christianity. Filled with the fervor of new converts, the young men set out for the

Holy Land. Along the way, tragedy struck. Venantius fell ill and died. Honoratus turned back. But he never returned home.

Instead, after stopping in Rome, Honoratus made a new home for himself on an uninhabited island off the coast of Provence that was known at the time as Lérins Island.

Word soon spread about the holy hermit living a life of prayer and penance on a Mediterranean island. Disciples sought him out, seeking solitude and prayer as a path to Christ. In time, a monastery was built on the island and a vineyard planted. Legend has it that, early on, so many snakes and spiders dwelt on the island, that they threatened the safety of Honoratus and his monks. In biblical fashion, the men worked tirelessly to construct a monastery tower, where they could be safe from the creatures. As soon as it was complete, a massive tidal wave washed in over the island. When it washed out, it took all the snakes and spiders with it, leaving only the monks, safe in their tower, behind.

That legend is questionable. Less questionable are the other legends surrounding the island.

One story says that Saint Patrick (before he was Saint Patrick) spent time on the island, training for his missionary work in Ireland.

That is possibly true.

Another story has Saint Hilary of Arles living and studying there before becoming the bishop of Arles. Since Hilary wrote the *Life of Honoratus*, that one is almost definitely true.

Hilary's *Vitae* tells us that Honoratus eventually left the island for the City of Arles, where the Church wanted him to serve as bishop. He consented only after receiving permission to continue guiding his monks from afar. After his death in 429 A.D., the island on which those monks lived came to be known by his name: Isle de Honoratus or, more commonly, Saint-Honorat.

The Abbaye was also the home of one of the great Fathers of the Church, St. Vincent of Lérins, who died there c. 445 A.D.

Parallel Worlds

For over a thousand years, Honoratus' community thrived on their island home, living according to the unique rule the saint had written for his first monks. They did struggle at times, most notably in 732, when the Saracens stopped there on their way to conquer parts of southern France. Although some monks escaped to safety, the monastery's abbot and several other brothers were slaughtered. During times of peace, however, the island was a popular place of pilgrimage, and the monks welcomed visitors from around the world.

More struggles came for the monks in the 12th and 13th centuries, when the Ottoman Turks rose to power and pirates threatened Europe's coastlines. To avoid meeting the same fate as their eighth-century abbot did, the monks built a fortified monastery to which they could retreat (and attack from) when invaders came to the island.

Ironically, it was the Catholic nation of Spain who, in 1635, was the first to succeed at expelling the monks from Saint-Honorat when they seized it during the Franco-Spanish wars. Two years later, the French seized it back, and the monks returned. They remained there until the French Revolution, when some of the monks were arrested and executed, while others escaped. The island and every building on it became government property for a time, until the early 19th century when it was sold to a French actress, who lived there for 20 years.

The island returned to Catholic hands in 1859, when a local bishop purchased it with the hope of handing it over to a religious order. It took 10 years to find one willing to take the project on, but eventually a group of Cistercians from Avignon agreed to settle there.

The Cistercians arrived in 1869, moved back into the old monastery, and, in short order, replanted the vineyard, orchard, and gardens, with every intention of living their life completely hidden from the world.

Shortly before their arrival, however, the British statesman Henry Peter Brougham bought property a few miles away from the island, in the mainland city of Cannes. There, Brougham built a beautiful home, then invited his friends to come visit. His friends liked Cannes so much that soon the British aristocracy were buying and building throughout the city.

By the end of the 19th century, trains were bringing Europe's wealthiest citizens to Cannes, where they stayed in luxury hotels, with no expense spared. Casinos were built in the early 20th century, and, not long before World War II began, the city council decided to start a film festival. Over 80 years later, that festival is still taking place every May, attracting more than 125,000 visitors to the city annually.

The Island of Saint Honorat is the second largest of the Lérins Islands, less than 1 mile long and 1,320 feet wide. It is only about 1 mile from the French mainland.

Mutual Benefit

Amid Cannes' explosive growth, the beautiful island less than four miles away did not escape notice. Curious tourists and pilgrims sailed across the waters — some to explore the ancient buildings, some to pray with the monks, some to do both. The monks in turn recognized that these visitors and the even greater number in Cannes might prove to be a good market for their wines. And so, a happy relationship began, with the monks welcoming visitors for Mass, pilgrimages, and tours, and the visitors supporting the monks' life of prayer by purchasing their wines.

As the years, passed, the wines of the Abbaye de Lérins grew in complexity and quality. So did their fame. A ferry began regularly-scheduled trips to the island to bring both the faithful and the connoisseurs to Saint-Honorat. A tasting room went up on the docks, as did a fine restaurant, where both the monks' wines and

The fortified monastery of Lérins was built in 1073 by Aldebert, the abbot of Lérins.

the dishes that best complement them could be served.

Today, 18 monks live on Saint-Honorat, and 10 of them are intimately involved in every stage of the winemaking process: manual harvest, pressing, fermenting, ageing, and bottling. In total, the monks produce six vintages — three red, three white — totaling 40,000 bottles per year.

Part of the wine's excellence is due to the island's *terroir* (growing environment), which is unlike any other in France. It's water-soaked soil, undergirded by limestone, possesses a high iron content from the ancient volcanoes. It also has one of the sunniest climates in Europe, with over 300 days of sun. Likewise, the sea breezes which waft across the island, gently deposit salty Mediterranean water on everything grown there, including the grapes, adding a mild saltiness to their natural sweetness. The primary vegetation on the island are olive trees and fir trees, with the latter encircling the Abbey's vines and protecting them from the harshest winds.

In total, eight hectares are under the vine on Saint-Honorat, producing Clairette, Chardonnay, Viognier, Syrah Mourvèdre, and Pinot Noir varietals.

Perhaps the most prized wine this *terroir* helps produce is the *Saint Pierre*. Served to the judges at Cannes every year, the wine is a blend of 70 percent Chardonnay and 30 percent Clairette. With notes of peaches, apples, and honey, the sweetness is balanced by its moderate acidity. Although the *Saint Pierre* tastes delicious with a Mediterranean salad with marinated calamari, its high alcohol content of 14.5 percent often calls for more food than just salad. Try it with quiche made with smoked salmon and goat cheese or with a Spanish paella.

Saint-Honorat's *Syrah* is an intense dark red, with hints of spicy black pepper balancing out the notes of red fruits. Powerful, well-structured, and with a long finish, the *Syrah* can hold its own with rich grilled meat, such as duck or lamb, barbeque beef, and for an unconventional pairing, a bahn mi sandwich.

Visiting Saint-Honorat

Throughout the year, ferries depart from the Port de Cannes to Saint-Honorat every hour. Visitors are encouraged to join the monks for prayer throughout the day or for Mass. They also can tour the grounds and historic buildings and chapels for free.

The monks also welcome individuals and groups for personal retreats throughout the year. Retreatants may stay for up to one week in the monks' guesthouse. There is no charge, but a free will offering is recommended, and some help with monastery duties (such as clearing the table after meals) is appreciated.

Wines can be enjoyed with lunch at the island's Restaurant la Tonnelle, or sampled in the vineyards with the monks on the first Friday of every month. Private tours and tastings can also be arranged for groups and organizations by contacting the monastery.

For more information:
E-mail: abbaye-contact@abbayedelerins.com
Telephone: 00 33 (4) 92 99 54 20
Website: www.AbbayedeLerins.com

CHATEAV
DV
CLOS DE VOVGEOT
MONVMENT HISTORIQVE
CHEF D'ORDRE DE LA CONFRERIE
DES CHEVALIERS DV TASTEVIN

Chateau Clos de Vougeot

Vougeot, France

In the French region of Burgundy, three renaissances took place. Two were renaissances of monastic life. One was a renaissance of viticulture. And all three were connected.

The Cluniac Movement

The first renaissance began in Cluny in the year 900.

After the disintegration of the Roman Empire, monasteries became the last remaining centers of learning and culture. Within their walls, monks preserved the books of Sacred Scripture, as well as the writings of the Church Fathers and ancient Greek philosophers. In their halls, missionaries were formed, who would eventually go forth to spread the Gospel to the peoples of Scandinavia, Eastern Europe, and the British Isles. And to the monasteries, as barbarian tribes launched one attack after another on the Empire's old cities and villages, peasants and gentry frequently fled, seeking safety within.

In time, virtual cities began to form within the monasteries, which offered shelter, medicine, and work to lay people in need of protection. By the eighth century, many monasteries were home to more laymen than religious, such as one Frankish monastery which, by the late seventh century, housed 700 people, only 300 of whom were religious brothers and priests.

As is the way with all things in a fallen world, however, with growth in size, wealth, and influence, came corruption. Vows were betrayed, the faith neglected, and worldly concerns increasingly trumped everlasting ones. Observing the mess that so many Benedictine monasteries in his native Burgundy had become, William I, Duke of Aquitaine, decided to try a new way of doing things. He believed independence offered the best way to protect a monastery from the corruption in both Church and state, so he endowed a new monastery in Cluny in 910. Rather than have Cluny's abbot answer to him or to the local bishop (as was usually done), however, he made the abbot answerable only to the pope.

That freedom enabled religious life at Cluny to flourish. And not just at Cluny. In the decades that followed, more than 1,000 "daughter houses" to Cluny sprang up across Europe. All lived according to the Benedictine Rule, and all worked to bring about a new springtime of the faith in Europe.

By the end of the 11th century, however, some Benedictine monks felt that more than what Cluny offered was needed. They wanted a life filled with more rigor, more penance, and more faithful adherence to the Rule of Saint Benedict. So, in 1098, a group of monks from the Cluniac monastery at Molesme broke with Cluny and established a monastery at Citeaux. They traded in their black Benedictine habits for white ones and adopted a more austere way of life, with a special emphasis on manual labor, especially agricultural labor.

They called themselves the Cistercians.

The Cistercian Movement

Fifteen years after the monastery at Citeaux was established, a young nobleman named Bernard came knocking at their door. Behind him stood 30 Burgundian noblemen, all friends and family members of Bernard's. Not only had Bernard made up his mind to join the Cistercians, but somehow he had persuaded almost everyone close to him to join as well.

In the years that followed, the Cistercians put Bernard's powers of persuasion (along with his deep faith and remarkable intellect) to good use. After he had been with them for just three years, his order sent him to establish a second Cistercian monastery at Vallée d'Absinthe, which Bernard named Claire Vallée, or Clairvaux. From there, Bernard went on to found 70 more Cistercian monasteries in his lifetime.

Those monasteries that Bernard established helped launch the second renaissance of faith and life that spread across Europe in the high Middle Ages. They also helped launch a renaissance in winemaking.

In the beginning, Bernard and his monks planted vineyards not to turn a profit for their order, but simply to provide wine for the sacred Liturgy. They weren't in a hurry to grow vast amounts of grapes, but they did want to grow good grapes, giving their best offering to God and giving Christ the best wine possible to transform into His own Blood.

So, they did their research. They made careful notes, shared what they learned between monasteries, experimented with different varietals in different areas, and slowly perfected the art of

winemaking, sparking a wine renaissance in Burgundy. Key to that renaissance were two concepts the Cistercians developed: *climats* and *clos*.

Climats are precise plots of land, distinguished from one another by the features of the soil and local growing climate. Through trial and error, the monks assigned different varietals to the *climats* best suited to helping the grapes reach the peak of their perfection. *Clos* are *climats* surrounded by walls. The monks built those walls to protect their vineyards from the local wildlife, but they ended up not only defining the growing areas, but also the names of the wines those areas produced.

For hundreds of years, the most famous and arguably greatest wine in the world produced by the Cistercian system of winemaking was *Clos Veugeot*. The great wine historian Desmond Seward, author of *Monks and Wine*, called it "the most remarkable of all achievements in the entire history of monastic viticulture."

Historical records lend credence to such a claim. Centuries earlier, in 1667, a monk refused to go make his case about some issue at his order's general chapter, because it was being held at Citeaux, where the abbot disagreed with him. "Why bother?" asked the monk, since "by lavishly entertaining all the abbots from Switzerland, Germany, Poland, and other foreign countries and pouring out vast quantities of his excellent *Clos Vougeot* … he will persuade them to do whatever he wants."

Preserving a Legacy

The first vineyard at Vougeot predates Bernard by three years. In 1110, a man named Guerric of Chamballe gave the white monks at Citeaux a small plot to farm. Slowly, the monks began acquiring more land in the area immediately surrounding that first plot, until, by 1336, they controlled 125 contiguous acres. They then surrounded that land with a *clos*, making it the largest vineyard in all of Burgundy. By the end of the 14th century, almost 50 laymen worked alongside the brothers there, tending the vines and making the wine.

To house their vast winemaking industry, the Cistercians built a *cuverie*, or vat house, with four giant winepresses and the Grand *Cellier*, an ingenious above-ground wine cellar. Later, in the mid-16th century, the 48th abbot of Citeaux, Dom Jean Lysier, decided he wanted to visit his vines and entertain guests there more often, so he built an elaborate chateau alongside an expanded grange.

All that was lost when revolution came to France. The Abbey at Citeaux was all but destroyed, and its possessions sold at auction. The grange, chateau, and vineyards at Clos Vougeot were bought by a banker, Gabriel-Jules Ouvrard, who in turn sold them to a wine-merchant, Léonce Bocquet, who saved as much as could be saved.

Over time, the 125 acres within the *clos* were subdivided and sold to different owners. The grange and chateau, however, remain, along with the ancient winepress first built by the Cistercians. They were restored and continue to be preserved by the *Confrérie des Chevaliers du Tastevin*, who hold dozens of events there annually to foster appreciation for the wines of Burgundy and the art of winemaking developed by the Cistercians.

Today, visitors can walk through the buildings erected by the Cistercians, tour the vineyards, and sample the wines grown

The medieval cverie *or vat house with four original winepresses.*

within the *clos*. The wines featured in the tastings vary from week to week, in order to feature as many local winemakers as possible.

While the monks grew both red and white grapes (mostly Pinot Noir and Chardonnay), today's *Clos Vougeot* wines are all reds, with intense colors ranging from strawberry to garnet. The typical *Clos Vougeot* will have a floral bouquet, with notes of blackberries, raspberry, wild mint, licorice, or even truffle, and a long finish. Most can be aged 10 to 30 years and often longer. If planning a meal with a *Clos Vougeot*, the wine is best showed off with savory starters such as *foie gras* or a strong Camembert cheese, or rich meats like roasted duck and roasted leg of lamb.

Visiting Chateau Clos de Vougeot

Visitors are welcome at the Chateau six days a week, Tuesday through Sunday. Tours must be scheduled in advance, with guided tours offered each day the Chateau is open. Each tour features a presentation on both the unique *climats* of Burgundy and the vineyards of the Clos Vougeot. Guests then take a self-guided tour through the Castle, 12th century winery, the old Cistercian cellars, and the old Cistercian dormitory. There, they can watch the film *"Jamais en Vain, Toujours en Vin" (*"Never in Vain, Always in Wine"*)* narrated in English by Julian Sands.

After the film, guests gather to sample five local wines. Reservations must be made in advance.

For more information:
E-mail: visites@closdevougeot.info
Telephone: +33 3 80 62 86 09
Website: www.ClosdeVougeot.fr/en/

The 14th-century cloister ruins of Les Cordeliers are a UNESCO World Heritage Site.

Les Cordeliers

Saint-Émilion, France

In the spring, summer, and fall, tourists from around the world fill the streets of Saint-Émilion. They come as pilgrims — of a sort — to the French village perched high atop a hill in the heart of Bordeaux.

Picking their way along the slippery, sloping cobblestone sidewalks which line the town's narrow medieval streets, these pilgrims move in and out of the wine shops housed in the limestone buildings of Saint-Émilion. The wine is what they have come to pay homage to. It is the lifeblood of both the village and the region, the red gold of Bordeaux. The finest wines in the world — *Petrus*, *Cheval Blanc*, *Ausone* — are grown in the shadow of the village, and the rarest and best of the vintages can be tasted and purchased in its shops.

The Hermit Saint

Eight hundred years ago, Saint-Émilion looked much as it does today. The limestone buildings standing now stood then, and its pilgrim-filled streets, likewise, were pilgrim-filled then. Those pilgrims, however, were a different sort of pilgrim. They were pilgrims come to pay homage to the holy man whose name the town bore: St. Émilion of Brittany.

According to local legend, during the mid-eighth century, St. Émilion served in the castle of a great nobleman in the north of France. Unbeknownst to his employer, Émilion had made a habit of smuggling bread out of the royal kitchen and into the hands

of the poor. One day, however, the great lord noticed something suspicious under his vassal's cloak. He demanded to know what this aspiring Robin Hood was carrying.

It was bread, of course, but, hoping to fool his employer, Émilion answered, "Only wood."

The lord called Émilion's bluff and ordered him to remove his cloak. Émilion drew back the folds. As he did, the loaves of bread were miraculously transformed into a bundle of firewood. Overwhelmed by God's grace, Émilion left Brittany and entered a Benedictine monastery. He remained there for six years, then set out on his own, seeking greater silence and solitude in the limestone caves that dotted the Aquitaine region.

He found neither. Not long after Émilion settled down in his stone hermitage, men and women began seeking him out. He baptized thousands of souls and heard the confessions of thousands more. Eventually, an entire Benedictine community grew up around Émilion's cave. Or, more accurately, grew down. When his monks weren't praying, they were digging, hollowing out the great limestone hill in which Émilion had sought refuge and shaping it into a church. Completed early in the 12th century, it remains the largest monolithic church in the world — 38 feet high, 64 feet wide, and 90 feet long — and although the Benedictine community was evicted after the French Revolution and never returned, local priests ensure that Holy Mass is still said there monthly.

Les Cordeliers

As the town of Saint-Émilion grew around the Benedictine church and monastery, other religious orders came to the area as well, including the Franciscans in the 13th century.

Although Saint Francis had founded his order with the intention of his men dedicating themselves to absolute poverty, possessing no buildings, lands, or even the funds to feed themselves, that intention passed away not long after Francis himself. Despite protracted protests from some of the friars, by the end of the 13th century, the Franciscans were building churches and monasteries across much of Europe.

It was around this time when the Franciscans arrived in Saint- Émilion. There, as in most of the rest of France, they were known as the *Cordeliers,* due to the long rope cord they wore around their waists.

In the beginning, the *Cordelier*s stayed outside the city, planting vineyards and building a church not far from the city gate. In the early 14th century, however, as the Hundred Years War heated up and resulted in the sacking of their home, the *Cordeliers* sought permission to move inside the city gates. Permission was granted, and, in 1338, the friars began building a new home behind Saint-Émilion's stone fortifications.

The Les Cordeliers Cloister Boutique

For almost 400 years, the building continued, with the friars perpetually adding on to their monastery. By the early 18th century, that friary included a dormitory, cloister, magnificent church, vineyard, vat room, cellar, and vegetable and herb garden.

All that building came to an end with the French Revolution. The *Cordeliers* themselves were banned and banished, and their 284 houses and monasteries across the country were seized by the state. The once lush vineyard lay fallow, and the walls began to crumble.

Nearly 60 years after the *Cordeliers* were driven out of France, the law changed, and the state permitted their return. Across the country, Franciscan friars returned to their old monasteries. But none returned to Saint-Émilion.

A Different Kind of Bordeaux

Not until the end of the 19th century, did a French winemaker by the name of Mr. Meynot purchase what had become a shell of the old Franciscan monastery. He was a good winemaker, but success in sales had always eluded him. This time, however, he wanted to try something new. He believed that the tunnels beneath the old monastery were exactly suited to aging St. Émilion wines in the style of Champagne. After making a careful study of the methods used in the Champagne region to make sparkling wines, Meynot followed suit, and, in 1892, began replicating the process with the wines of Bordeaux.

Meynot's theory proved correct, and his wines became an immediate success. Although the old monastery has had many owners in the decades since, all have continued to make sparkling wines in the monastery's underground tunnels. Those wines are currently sold under the name *Les Cordeliers*.

Today, Les Cordeliers produces a range of dry and semi-sweet sparkling wines, both white and rose. The varietals, including Cabernet Franc, Cabernet Sauvignon, Merlot, Semillion, Muscadelle, and Sauvignon Blanc, are brought in from vineyards outside the city walls, then bottled immediately after the alcoholic fermentation and blending. Bottles are all stored upside down and turned daily, which allows the yeasts to naturally create gas during a second fermentation. They are then aged a minimum of 12 months before the yeasts are disgorged. Each bottle is next topped off with *liqueur d'expédition* (base wine and sugar mixed) before it's corked and fitted with a wire cap.

The wines themselves are categorized as Prestige, Vintage, and Grand Vintage, with the Grand Vintage being the best Les Cordeliers wines, produced from the oldest and most exceptional vines. One of the more interesting of the Grand Vintages is the *Dry White*. Made from only Cabernet Franc, the wine has fine bubbles and a fruity bouquet with secondary hints of almond. Shot through with golden threads of color, the earthiness of the Cabernet Franc grape shines when paired with rich aperitifs, such as *foie gras* and prosciutto and figs or with spicier Indian dishes like lamb vindaloo.

One step down in the price range is the Vintage *Rosé*. This salmon-colored sparkling wine is fragrant with cherries and strawberries on the nose and raspberries on the palate. Full bodied, with a long, elegant finish, it is excellent with pan-fried salmon and roasted summer vegetables, as well as desserts made with summer fruits.

Visiting Les Cordeliers

From April through early November, tourists can visit the Franciscan monastery's former garden and cloister, along with a newer gift shop, for free during opening hours. In the gift shop, wine tastings are available, while picnic lunches and wine (by the glass or bottle) can be purchased at the on-site wine bar, then enjoyed on the cloister grounds. Guided tours are also available of the monastery's underground tunnels and cellar. In the spring and fall, a more extensive guided tour of Saint-Émilion and Les Cordeliers is also available via foot or motorized rickshaw. Tours can be booked at the Saint-Émilion Tourist Office or online.

For more information:
E-mail: contact@lescordeliers.com
Telephone: +33 05 57 24 42 13
Website: www.LesCordeliers.com

Rue
Dom
Pérignon
St Menehould 1638
arrive à
inventeur de la

Maison Drappier

Urrville, France

At Maison Drappier, a charming house and champagne cellar in the southernmost corner of the Champagne region, Benedictine and Cistercian history meet.

The Father of Sparkling Champagne

Like all modern-day makers of sparkling wine, Maison Drappier is in the debt of the Benedictines, who were the first to produce the drink that we know today as Champagne. Or, more specifically, they are in the debt of one particular Benedictine, Dom Perignon.

Born in 1638, in the eastern part of France's Champagne region, Perignon joined the Benedictines when he was just 19 . For about a decade, he lived and served at the Abbey of Saint Vanne at Verdun before, for reasons unknown to history, he transferred to the Hautvillers monastery near the river Marne in France. There, the monks regularly welcomed pilgrims, who came to pray for the miraculous intercession of the Emperor Constantine's mother, Saint Helena, whose body was entombed in the monastery's chapel.

Like the pilgrims, the monks also sought Saint Helena's intercession, crediting her prayers with the excellent grapes they grew on their 100 acres of fertile land.

By 1670, Perignon was the cellarer at Hautvillers and charged with managing the vineyard's finances and administration. He also was responsible for making sure the monastery's wine fetched the highest possible price. One way to do that was to improve the quality of the wines, so Perignon undertook an overhaul of the entire winemaking process at the Abbey.

He started by improving the wine cellars, digging deeper and wider cellars than any monks before him. He next began looking for a way to make the Champagne produced by the Abbey appear red, instead of the more common pinkish-grey color (*vin gris*) that marked the Champagne of the 17th century. He succeeded at that by using grapes from old vines, with more tender skin. That method, however, only worked during particularly sunny years.

So, Perignon next set out to find a way to make white wine from red grapes. He managed that by developing a new method of pressing his wines.

Perignon's innovations were paired with the careful selection and combination of grapes, developing new blends, not only according to the flavor of individual grapes, but also according to the weather each year. His methods worked. By 1690, Hautvillers' wines were famous, and, by 1694, they were fetching prices so high, the monks decided to etch the amount on their wine press.

Perignon wasn't done yet though.

Cistercian Vines

Thanks to the innovation of storing wine in glass bottles, which came into widespread use during his tenure at Hautvillers, Perignon began paying special attention to the second fermentation that caused a bubbling effect in certain wines. His goal was to capture the wine at a particular moment of aeration and preserve those bubbles. The problem was that the bottle stoppers of his day — wooden plugs wrapped in oil-soaked hemp — made that impossible.

Then one day, two Spanish monks came calling at the Abbey, and, while visiting with them, Perignon noticed they were drinking water from bottles with stoppers made of cork. That set him to experimenting, and soon enough Perignon swapped his wooden

plugs for cork plugs. By 1698, that switch made it possible for the Benedictine monk to produce the first great bottle of the sparkling wine that the world now knows as Champagne.

Within two years, the Champagnes from the Hautvillers Abbey were selling for twice as much as the very best still *vin gris* champagnes had once sold, and, within a decade, it was the preferred drink of kings, queens, and nobility throughout France and much of Europe.

Dom Perignon died in 1715 and was buried in the Abbey church of Hautvillers. His Abbey ceased to function as a monastery when the French Revolution came. His method for producing magnificent sparkling wine, however, endured, spreading across the Champagne region and beyond.

For that method, Maison Drappier remains in Perignon's debt. But for the land on which they grow their grapes, the cellars in which they age them, and even for some of the vines themselves, it is the Cistercians they have to thank.

Although the first vines were planted on Drappier land nearly 2,000 years ago, those disappeared with the end of the Roman Empire. Over half a millennium passed before the vineyards of Urrville were resurrected by Saint Bernard of Clairvaux. In 1152, he sent monks from the nearby Abbey at Clairvaux to plant vines and dig out new cellars to supply the Abbey with wine for both Mass and table. In quick order, more than 600,000 liters of wine

were produced on the property annually. That was far more than Bernard's monks needed, so much of it was casked and shipped in wooden barrels for sale.

That went on for over 600 years. Then, came the Revolution, followed by Napoleon Bonaparte, who turned the Clairvaux Abbey into a prison. Napoleon had no use for the cellars, though, and the local priests eventually moved into them, turning them into the presbytery. Around the same, the Drappier family arrived in Urrville. They purchased some of the land formerly owned by the Abbey and planted a small vineyard.

Slowly, the family expanded their landholdings, and, after World War II, was able to purchase the old Cistercian cellars and restore them to their original purpose. Within 20 years, they were producing champagnes so fine that France's great liberator from the Nazis and former president, General Charles de Gaulle, had become their most loyal customer, maintaining a continuous stock of his favorite Drappier bottles at his private residence.

A Family Business

Today, three generations of Drappiers run Maison Drappier, which in 2016 earned the unique distinction of becoming the first "carbon neutral" estate in the Champagne region. Nearly 2,000 square meters of solar panels provide 75 percent of the energy needed to run the estate, including powering their fleet of electric vehicles. The family has also designed and manufactured a more environmentally-friendly champagne bottle, which is 15 percent lighter than the average champagne bottle.

The vineyards themselves span 62 hectares and are dominated by Pinot Noir, which makes up 70 percent of the varietals grown there. Pinot Meunier (at 15 percent), Chardonnay (at nine percent), and old grape varieties (at six percent) make up the rest.

Unlike at many other estates, the Drappier wines are vinified with minimal intervention. There is no filtering or discoloring, and no animal products are used. The Drappiers are also passionate about producing champagnes without excessive use of sulfur. With some of the lowest amounts of sulfites in the industry, their champagnes are often marked by a natural deep gold or copper color.

Of the 12 cuvees produced by Maison Drappier, the most accessible and widely found is the *Carte D'Or*. Made from 80 percent Pinot Noir, 15 percent Chardonnay, and five percent Meunier, it has initial notes of peaches and nectarines, with a slightly spicy finish. It is ideal as an aperitif or with oysters or caviar.

To pay homage to the man who first had their vines planted, Maison Drappier has also created *Clarevallis*, named after Bernard of Clairvaux. Made from grapes grown on the first hillside planted at Urrville and vines descended from those of the Cistercian period, the *Clarevallis* is a blend of 75 percent Pinot Noir, ten percent Pinot Meunier, ten percent Chardonnay, and five percent Blanc

Vrai. The land on which these grapes grow is organically farmed and tilled, in part with a horse. A golden grey color, *Clarevallis* has a slight bitterness on the palate, with floral and berry notes. It beautifully balances a rich scallop risotto with brown butter sauce or boiled lobster.

Maison Drappier also produces two rosé champagnes, a champagne made from all white grapes, one made from all Pinot Noir, and one that is a blend of Chardonnay (25 percent) and "the forgotten grapes" — grapes once grown widely in the Champagne region, but which have long since fallen out of favor: Arbanne (25 percent), Petit Meslier (25 percent), and Blanc Vrai (25 percent). Named *Quattuor*, it is citrus-forward with a finish reminiscent of honeyed apples and fig jam. Marinated seafood and veal piccata pair well with it.

Visiting Maison Drappier

The Drappier family welcomes visitors to both the vineyards and cellars, providing personal tours and tastings. All tours are by reservation only.

For more information:
E-mail: info@champagne-drappier.com
Telephone: +33 03 25 27 40 15
Website: www.Champagne-Drappier.com/en/

Abbaye Sainte-Madeleine du Barroux

Le Barroux, France

As far as abbeys in France go, the Abbaye Sainte-Madeleine du Barroux (or Abbey of Le Barroux) in Provence is a relatively new one, both founded and built in 1970. Its wines, however, have a pedigree that go all the way back to Pope Clement V.

The Absentee Pope

In 1305, Clement became pope in what could politely be described as a less than holy way.

For about half a century before Clement's election, ever since Charles of Anjou did a major military favor for Pope Clement IV, the Bishops of Rome had been in the debt of the kings of France. Most of those bishops paid their debt by doing as the king asked. But not Pope Boniface VIII. He resisted French rule and instead tried to assert his spiritual authority over France's temporal leader. That ruler, Philip IV, didn't take kindly to Boniface's efforts and had the pope first deposed, then arrested. Boniface died in captivity. His successor, Blessed Benedict IX, reigned for only eight months and, after he too was less than accommodating to King Philip, died under circumstances so sudden and mysterious that murder was rumored. (Poisoning, to be exact.)

At the next conclave in 1305, the cardinals decided it was best to avoid electing any other pope who might run afoul of Philip's temper and chose instead one of the king's best friends: Raymond Bertrand de Got, Archbishop of Bordeaux, who took the name Pope Clement V.

After his election, the new Bishop of Rome made it clear that he had no intention of even visiting his diocese. At the time, Rome was known as a wild, dirty, riotous city, with a tendency to turn on its leaders (sacred and secular) and burn itself down periodically. Popes had been fleeing the city with the hopes of saving their lives for the better part of the 12th and the 13th centuries — taking up temporary residence in in nearby cities such as Naples, Perugia, and Viterbo — and Clement wanted no part of it.

For the first four years of his reign, Clement and the papal court resided in Poitiers. Then, he moved the court to the Comtat Venaissin, outside of Avignon. Today, the Comtat is part of the Provence-Alpes-Côte d'Azur region of France. At the time, however, even though the Comtat was surrounded by France, it technically belonged to the Papal States.

Clement reigned there as pope until 1314. In the between years, he made a mockery of the papacy. At the king's bidding, he sanctioned confessions obtained by torture and dissolved the Knights Templar in a successful attempt to seize their wealth. He also used his personal fortune (hundreds of millions in today's dollars) to finance war between France and England. When he died, it's said that lightning struck the church in which his body lay in state and burned him to ash.

After Clement, came another Frenchmen, John XXII. John would later be declared a heretic by his

The Abbey's location — at an altitude of 1,550 feet and surrounded by the foothills of Mount Ventoux and the Dentelles de Montmirail — makes for ideal growing conditions.

successor, Benedict II, for teaching that the blessed dead in Heaven do not behold the essence of God prior to Judgement Day. (Contrary to popular belief, popes absolutely can be heretics. They just can't define heresy as de fide doctrine.) Before all that, however, while John still lived and reigned, he built a gleaming stone palace along the Rhone River in Avignon. There, popes continued to reign until 1376, when Saint Catherine of Siena finally convinced Pope Gregory XI that no matter how bad the conditions in Rome might be, they weren't as bad as the conditions in hell. That ended the Avignon Papacy.

It did not, however, end the papal vineyards that Clement had planted outside of Avignon.

Forgotten Wines

In 1309, the same year Clement set up the papal court in the Comtat, he also found himself a lovely little summer place, about 20 miles outside of Avignon, at the foot of Mont Ventoux. There, at the Benedictine monastery of the Groseau in Malaucène, he had a vineyard planted. The straw wine ultimately produced by this vineyard became a papal favorite and was used to entertain visitors to both the monastery and the papal palace in Avignon for decades.

After the popes left, the vine growing and wine making continued, but other regions' wine quickly surpassed that of the Provence-Alpes-Côte d'Azur region in popularity, and the wine was mostly enjoyed locally. Not until after World War I did local wine-growers begin enhancing the *terroir* with the hopes of cultivating finer, more widely-recognized wines.

In 1973, their hard work paid off, and they received the much sought-after status of "AOC Ventoux" (Protected Designation of Origin). After that, they expected more recognition and more demand for their wines. Unfortunately, all that came was more struggle. Growing grapes on small, mountainous, rocky plots of land was easy for no one. Individual growers also struggled to make their wine efficiently, with mechanization neither affordable nor realistic for them given the size of their operations. Many couldn't stay in business, and land was abandoned, which only meant more struggle for those who stayed.

Then, in 2015, the monks of Barroux Abbey stepped in.

At the time, the Abbey was celebrating its 45th birthday. A group of traditional monks had founded the community in the years immediately following the Second Vatican Council. The monks were concerned with the direction of Catholic liturgy and life in the early years after the Council and hoped that by establishing a

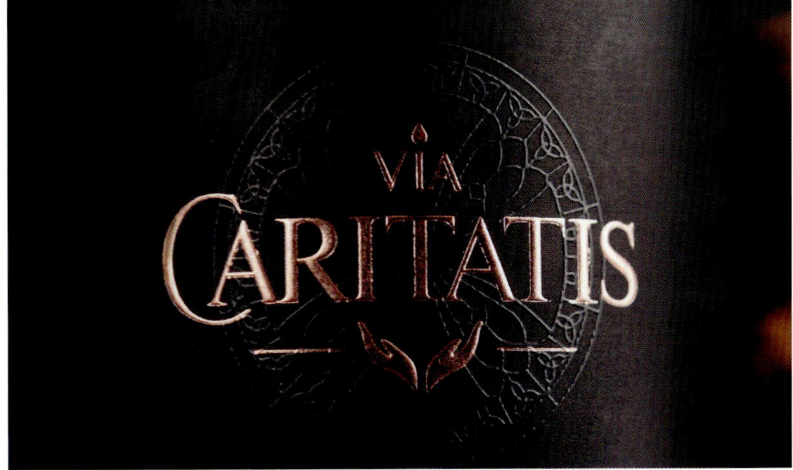

new monastery where the old liturgy was still offered, they could help preserve some of the quickly disappearing traditions for future generations. Nine years after their founding, they helped establish a sister house of Benedictine nuns nearby: the Abbey of Notre-Dame-de-l'Annonciation.

Although the monks and nuns of Barroux initially supported the work of Archbishop Marcel Lefebvre, they broke with him once he broke with the Church in 1988. The monks then sought and received permission from the Holy See to continue offering the Traditional Latin Mass. A year later, in 1989, the monastery church was elevated to the rank of an abbey.

Following the Benedictine tradition, the monks supported their life of prayer at the Abbey through manual labor — growing wheat, olives, and grapes, which they used to make bread, olive oil, and wine.

In 2015, however, as more and more local winemakers struggled to keep their operations afloat, the Abbey decided that perhaps they could help. They reached out to their neighbors and proposed forming a cooperative, which would allow them to pool resources, invest more heavily in equipment, and more actively research the best ways to cultivate their land and vines. Their neighbors responded enthusiastically, and Via Caritatis was born.

Via Caritatis

Today, Via Caritatis produces nine red, white, and rosé wines, subdivided into four categories. Three of those categories bear names which evoke different aspects of the Benedictine liturgy: Vox (Voice or Song), Pax (Peace), and Lux (Light). The fourth category, the Wines Abbayes, includes the Abbey's finest wines. On every label, across all four categories, Via Caritatis emblazon an image of two hands coming out from the earth and opening toward the sky, along with the words Via Caritatis and a rose window with a cross in its center, to remind those purchasing the wine of the path to which God calls them. A message printed on the cork drives that message home: *S'ils n'ont pas la charité, ils ne sont rien* ("If I do not have love, I am nothing," 1 Cor 13).

Notable among the *Pax* wines is the red, which is a blend of Grenache (85 percent) and Syrah (15 percent) and resembles the *Châteauneuf-du-Pape* wines, also grown in Provence. Deep maroon in color, with rich notes of caramel and licorice, it is warm and spicy on the palate, with a peppery finish. This bold wine pairs wonderfully with barbecued beef or a filet mignon with mushroom sauce.

The award-winning *Lux Rosé* is a secret and complex blend, with initial hints of citrus and peach, followed by berries, and ending with a lingering sweetness. It is lovely alongside soft cheeses like brie and goat, a cheese tortellini tossed with pesto and parmesan, or grilled vegetable pizza.

The finest of the wines are the Wines *Abbayes,* which are made exclusively by the monks and nuns and grown on land farmed solely by them. To offer the most benefit to every Via Caritatis partner, however, the Wines *Abbayes* can only be purchased in a box that includes wines from other local growers. The best of the best is the *Abbaye Red*, a bold, dry wine, with medium tannins and high acidity. On the nose, it has a floral bouquet and, on the palate, hints of sour cherry and gooseberry. Winter soups, like pumpkin soup, or a butternut squash and sausage risotto can bring out the best in the *Abbaye Red.*

Visiting Barroux Abbey

Although at this time the Abbey does not do wine tours or tastings, visitors are welcome to join the monks daily for the chanting of the Divine Office and the Extraordinary Form of the Mass, then visit the gift shop where they can purchase the wines, as well as bread and other treats to enjoy on the Abbey grounds.

To preserve their life of silence, the Abbey prefers all people interested in visiting contact them via a form available on their website: **www.barroux.org**.

Domaine Laroche
CHABLIS PREMIER CRU
2009
LAROCHE
Domaine Laroche
CHABLIS PREMIER CRU
2010
LAROCHE
Domaine Laroche
2010
Domaine Laroche
CHABLIS

DOMAINE LAROCHE

CHABLIS, FRANCE

In life, the patron saint of wine making, Martin of Tours, never visited the *Obédencerie de Chablis.* His only visit (of a sorts) to the former monastery in Burgundy came 400 years after his death. But there, his contributions to the art of viticulture are honored still.

The Patron Saint of Wine Making

Saint Martin's story begins around 316, with his birth in what is now Hungary. His father was a senior officer in the Roman army, and when Martin was 15 , Roman law required he join the army as well. Intelligent, disciplined, and capable, Martin quickly moved up through the ranks, becoming part of the emperor's elite personal guard by age 18.

It was during this time, that one day, while out on patrol, Martin came across a poor man, shaking with cold. Rather than see the man suffer, he took his warm soldier's cloak, cut it in two with his sword, and gave one half to the beggar. That night, in a dream, Martin saw Christ wearing the other half of the cloak. When he awoke, his cloak was whole again. Martin was only a catechumen at the time, but after that he firmly resolved to get baptized.

Once his period of service came to an end, Martin left the army and became a hermit. He also studied under the future Doctor of the Church, St. Hilary of Poitiers. Later, reportedly against his will, Martin became bishop of Tours. As the story goes, the people of Tours wanted Martin for their new bishop but knew he would never consent to visit if he suspected that they planned to elect

him. So, on the day of the episcopal election, a group lured him to the city under false pretenses. When Martin arrived and discovered what they were up to, he ran and hid in a barn. Unfortunately for him, the geese with whom he had temporarily taken up residence began honking so loudly at his presence that Martin was soon found and (reluctantly) ordained.

As bishop, Martin never abandoned the ways of a hermit and scandalized the nobles of his diocese with his ragged, unkempt appearance. Nevertheless, he was a faithful shepherd, who combatted Arianism, traveled routinely to even the most far-flung Christian communities in his care, and established numerous monasteries. It was due to events that occurred during those travels that winemakers eventually took him as their patron saint.

Although Martin forbade his monks from drinking wine for their own refreshment, they still needed wine for the celebration of the Mass. To this end, legend has it that Martin introduced the Chenin Blanc grape to the Touraine region, first planting it at one of his monasteries, then cultivating it and sharing cuttings with his other monasteries during his travels throughout the Loire Valley.

Another legend claims that Saint Martin, with the help of his donkey, discovered the importance of pruning vines. While traveling through France visiting his monasteries, he stopped at one for the evening, leaving his donkey tied in the vineyards. During the night, the donkey grew hungry and decimated the vines. Martin didn't discover what the beast had done until the next morning. Horrified, he apologized profusely to the monks. Months later, though, when springtime came, the monks discovered that the vines seemingly destroyed by the donkey's midnight snack were the healthiest in the vineyard. And thus, pruning the vines became standard in Martin's monasteries everywhere.

Master Winemakers

Those legends may or may not be true (odds are against his donkey inventing pruning). Regardless, by the ninth century, the monasteries first established by Martin of Tours were indeed using the Chenin Blanc grape to make some of the best wines of their day, with the Carolingian emperor Charles the Bald mentioning them in a document around A.D. 845.

It's also certain that almost 500 years after Martin's death, a small group of monks from his monastery in Tours went to Burgundy to found a new house in Chablis. Construction on the *Obédencerie de Chablis* began in 867. Along with building a dormitory and chapel, the monks planted a vineyard, dug out wine cellars, and built a wine press.

Ten years later, in 877, Norman armies threatened the Tours region. Fearing for the safety of Saint Martin's relics, which had been preserved in the Tours chapel since his death, the abbot of Tours entrusted the relics to one of his monks and ordered him to smuggle them off to the remote and well-hidden *Obédiencerie*. There, what remained of Saint Martin stayed for about a decade, until Tours was once again safe.

As the centuries passed, the *Obédiencerie* continued to grow. So did its reputation as a maker of fine wines. Written records of their excellence date to as early as 1128, and records marveling at the technological advances of their wine press date to 1216.

Family Laroche

For 900 years, life and winemaking continued with little change for the monks at Chablis. Then, came the French Revolution. The monks were evicted, and their buildings and vineyards put up for auction. The monastery passed into private hands, and, for a time, wine making at the *Obédiencerie* was no more.

In 1985, however, almost two centuries after the monks left the *Obédencerie*, the Laroche family purchased the ninth-century monastery to use as the headquarters of their century-old winemaking enterprise. They were already farming a sizable portion of the monk's old vineyards and saw great potential for aging their wines in the cellars first dug for the fruit of those vines over a thousand years earlier. So, the building was turned into office space, and the cellars cleaned up and reequipped. The 12th-century wine press (which has been declared a National Historic Monument) was likewise preserved.

Today, Domaine Laroche owns a total of nearly 90 hectares across the region. Each vineyard parcel is cared for by one person, who takes full responsibility for every aspect of cultivation on the plot, from pruning and soil conditioning, to control of yields and the sorting of the harvest. The goal at each plot is to focus on a low-yield harvest that produces the purest example of the grapes for each *terroir*.

Unlike in other parts of Burgundy, the cool climate of Chablis

combined with the region's unique Kimmeridgian soil — a mixture of clay, chalk, and fossilized oyster shells — produces a Chardonnay grape with more acidity and less fruitiness. The result is a wine with a dry, mildly metallic flavor.

By law, no other grapes than Chardonnay can be included in Chablis. Nevertheless, due to different exposures, vine quality, and aging methods, Domaine Laroche produce 16 distinct wines, including 10 premier crus and four grand crus. They also make an annual wine in honor of the saint to whom the *Obédiencerie* owes its existence: the *Chablis St. Martin*.

Both incredibly popular and highly rated, the *Chablis St. Martin* is a dry, elegant wine with a subtle bouquet of green apples and pears. Green apples are also evident on the palate, along with lemon and honey. The wine is best if left to age for at least two to three years and makes either an excellent aperitif or a pleasant companion to roasted salmon with lemon butter, grilled shrimp, or soft cheeses.

Among the grand crus, the *Les Bouguerots* is perhaps most notable. Made from grapes grown near the Serein River, on old vines selected and transplanted to this specific *terroir*, *Les*

Bouguerots is a bold, well-structured Chablis. With strong notes of lemon, butter, honey, and citrus, along with hints of chalk and pear, this wine should be left to age at least five to eight years. It shines when served with dishes such as lobster salad, veal piccata, and chicken with orzo, lemon, feta, and herbs.

Visiting Domaine Laroche

Domaine Laroche has a variety of touring packages for those wishing to learn more about the *Obédencerie*, Laroche wines, and the wines of Burgundy. One package includes a one-hour tour of the *Obédencerie*, a walk through the ancient cellars, and an examination of the monks' once great wine press, followed by a tasting of the cru wines. Visitors also can choose from tour packages that include lunch or dinner at partner restaurants in Chablis, a cycling tour of the vineyards (with a box lunch provided), and a two-day immersion tour, with meals, overnight accommodations, and tours of two Burgundian wineries. Reservations required.

Along with the tours, the *Obédencerie* also operates a small shop, where visitors can peruse the winery's offerings and purchase a few bottles to take home.

For more information:
E-mail: boutique@larochewines.com
Telephone: +33 03 86 42 89 28
Website: www.larochewines.com/en

SPAIN

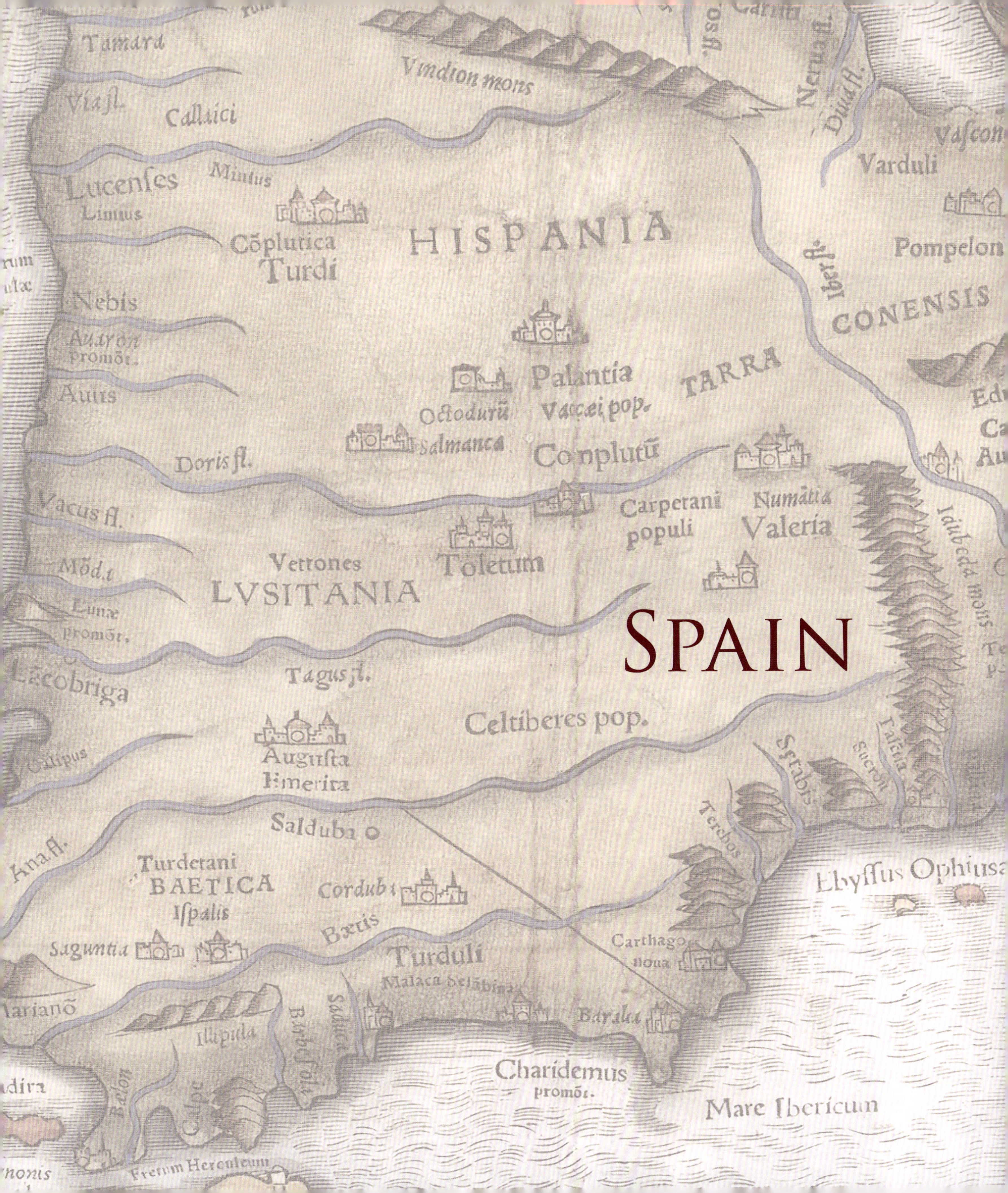
Tamara
Vindion mons
Via fl.
Callaici
Lucenses
Minius
Limius
Cõplutica
Turdi
HISPANIA
Nebis
Auaron promõt.
Auus
Palantia
Vaccæi pop.
Octodurũ
Salmanca
TARRA
Cõplutũ
Doris fl.
Vacus fl.
Carpetani populi
Numãtia
Valeria
Vettrones
Toletum
LVSITANIA
Mõd.
Lunæ promõt.
Tagus fl.
Celtiberes pop.
Augusta Emerita
Salduba
Turdetani
BAETICA
Ispalis
Cordubi
Bætis
Saguntia
Turduli
Malaca
Carthago noua
Charidemus promõt.
Mare Ibericum
Ebyssus
Ophiusa
Varduli
Pompelon
Iber fl.
CONENSIS
Idubeda mons
Sucron
Fretum Herculeum
Illipula

Cellars De Scala Dei

Terragona, Spain

In 1194, local legend claims that a small group of Carthusian brothers from Provence came to Spain, looking for a location to establish a new monastery. Their needs were simple: water and isolation.

The brothers' search eventually led them to the foothills of the Montsant range, where they encountered a shepherd working in the wilderness. Upon seeing the Carthusians, the shepherd recalled a recent dream, in which he had seen a staircase stretching from Heaven down to the field where he tended his sheep. In the dream, the shepherd saw angels ascending the staircase, entering Heaven. He told the Carthusians of the dream. For them, that settled the matter; they would build their monastery there, in that very field.

God's Ladder

Whether or not that legend is true, the small community of Carthusians did indeed build a monastery (or "charterhouse") in the foothills of the Montsant mountains, not far from the Mediterranean coast. In a nod to the shepherd's dream, they named it *Scala Dei,* meaning "God's ladder."

There, following the rule of Carthusian life established by the order's founder — the 11th-century saint Bruno of Cologne — the monks lived in almost complete solitude. Each abided in their own small dwelling, where they spent the day engaged in prayer and labor. Each monk also had his own small garden connected to his hut, where he could pray and grow vegetables or flowers. All week, the

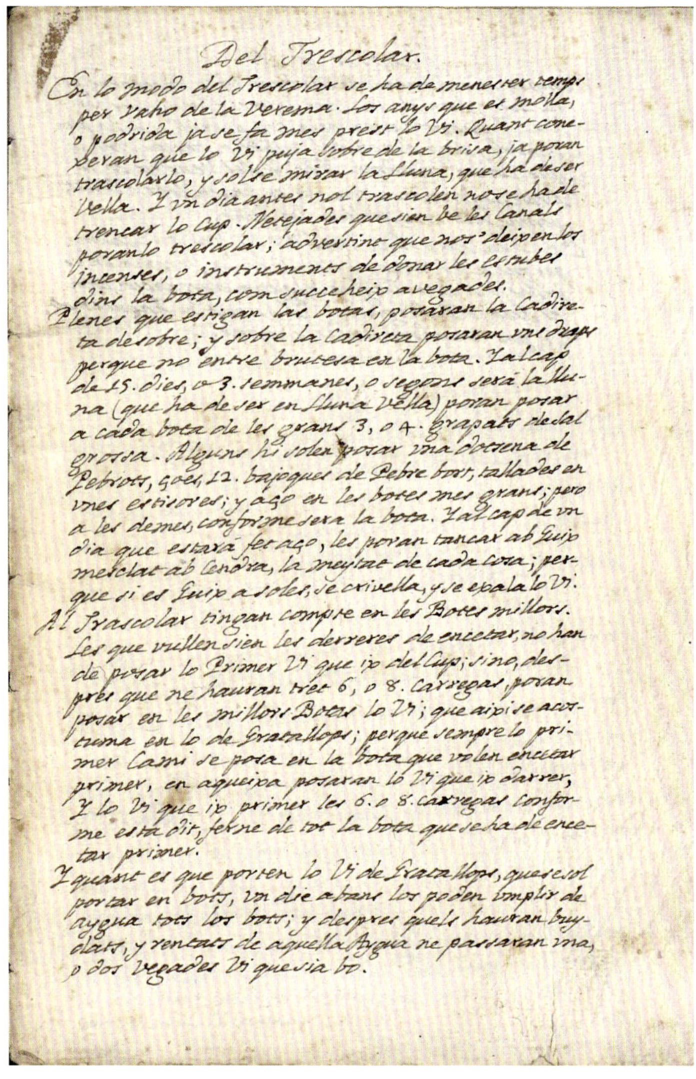
Del Trescolar.

Original document from the Sociedad Agrícola La Unión, *founded in 1844.*

monks refrained from speaking, engaging in only brief conversation on Sundays, during a set time for community recreation.

Unlike most monastic communities, Carthusian monks pray portions of the Liturgy of the Hours on their own, leaving their cell and joining their brothers only three times a day. Other than Sundays, when they dine in community, the monks' two daily meals are taken alone in their cell. Those meals are prepared and brought to them by the lay brothers, who see to the monastery's physical needs, from cooking and chopping wood to doing laundry and repairing the monastery.

At Scala Dei, those lay brothers also worked with local farmers to turn the remarkable grapes produced by the red clay soil and long, hot, dry summers into an even more remarkable wine.

The Era of Confiscations

As the years passed, due in no small part to their wine, Scala Dei grew in size and wealth, eventually owning thousands of acres of lands and ruling over every village for miles. For this reason, the region became known as the Priorat, taking its name from the Carthusian Prior who ran the charterhouse (Carthusians were governed by Priors, not Abbots). It was to the Prior that the local inhabitants paid the dreaded *diezmo* — a punishing tax on their crops — and the Prior, far more than any faraway king, ruled over them.

As the 18th century turned into the 19th century, the peasants' anger at the *diezmo* grew. At the same time, resentment among Spain's ruling class at the enormous wealth and landholdings of the country's religious orders also grew. Eventually, in 1835, the government passed the Ecclesiastical Confiscations of Mendizábal, allowing the state to dissolve all monasteries and convents and seize all their land and property. Like elsewhere in Spain, the monks and brothers of Scala Dei were cast out of their home, and their land was sold off to wealthy noblemen and merchants. Spain then used the proceeds from the sale to pay their enormous military debts.

Few peasants wept when the monks left. For all their prayers and piety, the monks of Scala Dei had not been kind to the local farmers, taxing them annually without exception and showing no mercy during hard years. Within two years of the monastery's dissolution, the once great charterhouse was in ruins, a victim to constant acts of vandalism by the locals, who took out their frustration on the departed monks by setting fires and sacking the buildings.

Nine years after the last Carthusian monk left Scala Dei, the monastery buildings and large tracts of the Carthusian vineyards were purchased by five families determined to continue making the region's famous wine. They called themselves the *Sociedad Agrícola La Unión*. Slowly, steadily, they brought the old vineyards back to life and began making wines in the monastery's former buildings. By 1878, they produced a wine good enough to win a gold medal at the Universal Exhibition in Paris. When the next Universal Exhibition was held 10 years later, this time in Barcelona, they won again.

But then the bottom fell out on the Spanish wine industry. The loss of colonial markets and the devasting Phylloxera plague, which wiped out countless vineyards across Europe, were partly responsible for the collapse. So was a global recession that led to significant price drops. Many winemakers, including the *Sociedad Agrícola La Unión*, ceased to exist. Near-constant wars in the early 20th century, starting with World War I, then the Spanish Civil War, and finally World War II didn't help, nor did massive depopulation in the region.

Scala Dei's cellars date from the 17th century and are still in use.

The surrounding Montsant mountain range.

The slate soil contributes to the unique growing conditions.

The Cellars de Scala Dei

Despite the local and global unrest, a few farmers continued struggling along, growing what they could, making what they could, and all the while fighting for recognition for the wines of the Priorat region. Finally, in 1954, the much-coveted status of D.O. (Designation of Origin) was granted to Priorat wines.

Twenty years later, in 1974, the Cellars de Scala Dei moved into the old monastery stables and began making their wine. Since then, they have slowly acquired 40 plots of land, including the plots formerly planted by the monks. Each is managed separately, to maximize the effects of the plots' unique soil composition and altitude on the grapes. Those grapes include Garnacha, Cariñena, Syrah, and Cabernet Sauvignon. Forty percent of Scala Dei's grapes are grown in red and yellow clay. The remaining 60 percent grow in schist, a soil comprised of hard, dense rocks layered with minerals that retain heat well and contribute to the big, bold flavors of Priorat reds.

The winemaking facilities of Cellars de Scala Dei are now located in the former stables of the charterhouse. There, wines ferment in open vats, enhancing the clean, fruity aromas of the Priorat wines. For the younger wines, that fermentation takes place in steel tanks, but the highest-quality wines (especially those coming from the monks' former plots) ferment in cement. Aging takes place in concrete barrels.

Currently, Scala Dei produces 11 wines: eight reds, two whites, and one rosé. One of their entry-level wines, the *Scala Dei Garnatxa*, is sourced from grapes grown on slate and red clay soils. Fresh and fruity on the palate, with a bouquet of Mediterranean herbs, it is excellent served with beef tartare, fried cauliflower, or chorizo sausage.

At the other end of the price spectrum, they offer *Scala Dei St. Antoni*, which is made exclusively from grapes grown in a high-altitude vineyard first planted during the time of the Carthusians. Bearing a notable resemblance to wines made of Pinot Noir, this Garnacha wine has one of the cellars' highest alcohol contents (14.5 percent), yet still tastes refined and delicate, with raspberry and wild strawberry fruit notes and graceful tannins. Herb roasted chicken, lamb biryani, and fried artichokes all complement the *St. Antoni*.

Another notable Scala Dei wine is its (relatively) new white Priorat, *Massipa de Scala Dei*. This high-altitude blend of Garnacha Blanca and Chenin Blanc is co-fermented in cement tanks, before ageing in *foudres* (large wooden vats). This white has a stony intensity, with citrus and wildflower notes, a hint of beeswax, and a long, powerful finish. A white that ages well, it pairs well with Maryland-style crab cakes, spaghetti *aglio e olio* with anchovies, or roasted cauliflower.

Visiting Scala Dei

Cellars de Scala Dei welcomes visitors seven days a week, offering tours in English lasting about 90 minutes and concluding with a sommelier-guided tasting of four wines. The winery also offers a tasting of three wines, with no tour. Those can be booked online in advance.

The Cellars Scala Dei ceded the ruins of the old Carthusian charterhouse to the Catalonian government in 1991, so tours of the monastery must be booked separately, through www.turismepriorat.org.

For more information:
Telephone: +34 977 82 71 73
E-mail: info@cellersdescaladei.com
Website: www.CellersdeScalaDei.com/en

Ruins of the Carthusian monastery and charterhouse of Santa Maria de Escaladei at Scala Dei, now a Catalonian historical monument.

HERAS CORDÓN

FUENMAYOR, SPAIN

Heras Cordón was never a monastery. The vineyards in which its grapes grow were never planted by saints. But the wines produced in the La Rioja winery still have a special connection to the Catholic Church.

The Pope's Wine

In 2001, the time had come for the Vatican to sign a new contract with its regular supplier of Rioja wine. The Spanish red, from what is arguably the country's most famous wine-growing region, was a favorite not only of the pope, but of the Vatican curia who regularly dined with him. That year, however, for reasons unknown, Pope St. John Paul II decided the time had come to pick a new Rioja. To make things fair, he announced that a tasting contest would be held. Whoever won the contest, would win the contract.

When the tasting was done, Heras Cordón winery was the winner. And, ever since 2001, it has remained the exclusive supplier of Rioja wine to the Vatican, with both Popes Benedict XVI and Francis renewing the contract (and one hopes Pope Leo XIV!).

Pope Benedict especially was known to be a fan of Rioja. In 2013, during a meeting with the tribunal of the Roman Rota, he greeted the judges one by one, with each judge introducing himself to the Holy Father and receiving a friendly nod in return. But when the judge from La Rioja presented himself, the pope broke with custom, proclaiming, "Oh, from La Rioja. Very good wine!"

All Heras Cordón wines bound for the Vatican are labeled with the personal crest of the pope and the Latin phrase *Misericordias Domini in aeternum cantabo* ("I will sing the mercies of the Lord forever"). Once labeled and crated, the wine goes to a small altar in the corner of the cellars, where a local priest blesses it before shipping. The altar itself carries a papal blessing.

The rest of Heras Cordón's wine is shipped around the world and is widely-recognized as one of the best wines of its region.

Post-War Boom

Winemaking in the La Rioja region likely dates to the Phoenicians in 800 B.C., but the earliest known vineyards were there at the latest by A.D. 873 , in connection with the San Andrés de Trepeana Monastery. In La Rioja, like elsewhere in Europe, it was usually the monks who made the finest (and most abundant) wine.

By the 13th century, La Rioja wines were being exported for sale, with wealthy nobles and churchmen across Europe prizing the unique wines produced in the northern Spanish climate. And by the 19th century, the Heras Cordón family had entered the wine business, constructing their first cellars in Lapuebla de Labarca in Rioja Alavesa.

For nearly a century, Heras Cordón was the smallest of family businesses, primarily growing grapes and making wine for local consumption. For many years, they didn't even bottle their wine, but rather sold it in bulk.

In the 1930s, with the onset of the Spanish Civil War, all production stopped. By 1940, however, the winery was back in business. After World War II, a country-wide focus on modernization led to the expansion of Heras Cordón's facilities. They also began aging their wines in French oak barrels for the first time.

By the 1970s, the family was selling its wine on the national market, and three decades of steady growth eventually led to the purchase of more vineyards and the construction of a new winery in Fuenmayor.

Tasting Rioja

Built from stones taken from old railway stations and with a massive front door rescued from an ancient monastery that had fallen into ruin, the current Heras Cordón winery looks as if it has stood for hundreds of years. Located in the middle of one of its many vineyards, the winery also contracts with local farmers to secure the necessary number of grapes each year. The vineyards are spread out across La Rioja, divided between Rioja Alta (Cenicero, Fuenmayor, and Navarrete) as well as Rioja Alavesa (Laguardia, Elciego, and Lapuebla de Labarca).

The primary varietals grown in the Heras Cordón vineyards are Tempranillo, Mazuelo, and Graciano. Heras Cordón handpicks those grapes, then blends them into nearly a dozen wines, including *Vendimia Seleccionada*, *Reserva*, and *Expresión*.

The *Vendimia Seleccionada* is Heras Cordón's most affordable wine and the wine the Vatican orders the most of annually. Comprised of 80 percent Tempranillo, 10 percent Mazuelo, and 10 percent Graciano, the wine is first fermented in stainless steel tanks, then aged for 13 months in American oak barrels. A bright cherry-colored, medium-bodied wine, it has initial notes of vanilla, cocoa, and red berries, followed by fainter notes of sandalwood. On the mouth, raspberry and plum flavors mingle with hints of chocolate and roasted coffee beans, making it the perfect pairing for savory Manchego cheese, meatier dishes like Texas chili, or the spicy, tomato-based pasta arrabiata.

The more refined *Reserva* is comprised of 90 percent Tempranillo, five percent Mazuelo, and five percent Graciano. After fermenting in stainless steel barrels, the wine is aged for 18 months in barrels made from both French and American oak. Fragrant with notes of cherry, red currant, and pink pepper, the *Reserva* is dry, with mild tannins, notes of cloves, blackberries, and cherries, and a finish reminiscent of coffee and toffee. The *Reserva* is the perfect complement to beef tenderloin or barbecue, as well as strong sheep cheeses, like pecorino.

The finest of the Heras Cordón wines is the *Expresa*, which is made almost entirely out of Temparanillo and aged exclusively in French oak for 22 months. With a rich garnet color, this full-bodied wine is fragrant with wild herbs, clove, cinnamon, and nutmeg. Fruity on the palate, with lively tannins, it has a long, creamy finish. It makes an excellent accompaniment to lamb chops crusted in herbs, Iberian ham, or venison stew.

Visiting Heras Cordón

Heras Cordón winery is open Monday through Saturday. Guests are welcome to visit the onsite store or reserve one of their extensive tours and tastings.

The tours, which are available in both English and Spanish, last up to six hours. They include a visit to the vineyards and cellars, followed by a meal of traditional Rioja dishes and a wine tasting. The meal and tasting both take place in the winery's luxuriously outfitted dining room, which is also made available to members of the vineyard's "bottle club."

For more information:
E-mail: tienda@herascordon.com
Telephone: +34 941 451 413
Website: herascordon.com

THE ROYAL ABBEY OF SANTA MARIA DE POBLET

POBLET, SPAIN

At the foot of the Prades Mountains, in a Catalonian hamlet so small you'll miss it if you blink while driving past, stands an ancient Abbey, where kings and queens once lived. Today, after spending a century in ruin, the Abbey is a functioning monastery once more, and the vineyards that surround its walls are again bursting with fruits destined for transformation in the Abbey's winery.

The hamlet in question, Poblet, is home to one of the largest, most magnificent monasteries in Spain, but not much else. Besides the monastery, all you'll find there is a handful of buildings and one lone café. Situated in the south of Catalonia, in the northeast corner of the Iberian Peninsula, the village exists almost as an extension of the Royal Abbey of Santa Maria de Poblet, which was built by French Cistercians in the mid-12th century.

A Christian Catalonia

Four hundred years earlier, in 711, over 12,000 Muslim troops from Tangiers defeated the Visgothic king Roderic in a great battle for control of the Iberian Peninsula. A few years later, a second battle ensured that two-thirds of the Peninsula was under Muslim control. Despite repeated attempts to retake the land, it remained in Muslim hands for the better part of the next 400 years.

The reconquest of Spain by Christian leaders didn't end in 1151, but by that year Christian forces had managed to displace Muslims from much of Catalonia. Catalonia's ruler at the time, Ramon Berengar IV, Count of Barcelona, believed that if he could repopulate the land with Christians, he might be able to prevent the Muslims from coming back. So, he started those repopulation efforts with monks.

At his invitation, Cistercians from France established three monasteries at key points in the newly-named Catalonia region. Thanks to the evangelical fervor of Saint Bernard of Clairvaux, the Cistercians' numbers had been exploding in France, so various monasteries had more than a few monks to spare.

The monks began building in Poblet in 1151, on land donated to them by Ramon. Around the same time, they planted vineyards for continuing the Cistercian tradition of winemaking. Into those vineyards they introduced the Pinot Noir grape, which their fellow Cistercians were growing in France with great success. Despite not being native to the region, the Pinot Noir thrived in Poblet, due to its long hot days and cool nights.

The King's Abbey

As the centuries passed, the Abbey grew in size and grandeur, with the final major additions built in the 16th century. By then, various workshops, storehouses, and worker accommodations, plus a chapel, were located immediately behind the monastery gates. A chapel and hospital for the poor stood in the middle enclosure, and, behind a fortified wall, in the innermost enclosure, the monks built their cloister, dormitory, library, and a great Gothic basilica, which dates to the 12th century. Also, within the innermost enclosure, behind defensive towers, the kings of Aragon built their royal residence, where their families stayed during their frequent visits to the Abbey.

The slate soil [illegible] to the [illegible] growing conditions.

Those visits increased after 1196 when, starting with Alfonso II (Ramon's son), all the kings of Aragon were buried in the Poblet Basilica. During his coronation, Peter IV of Aragon even made a solemn oath that all the Aragonese kings would be buried there. So they were, for 300 years, until Ferdinand II broke with tradition in 1516, choosing instead to be buried in Granada, with his wife, Queen Isabella.

In 1835, following the Ecclesiastical Confiscations of Mendizábal, which stripped the Cistercians of their ancient home, those tombs were among the first places desecrated by the mob which descended on the monastery as soon as the monks left. All the paintings and furniture were stripped from the building, fires set throughout, and many of the records of the Aragon kings lost. The local clergy did manage to eventually rescue the royal bodies and smuggle them to the diocesan cathedral for safekeeping, but not all bodies were kept intact.

For years, the monastery lay in ruins, its walls crumbling and its roofs collapsing. Some work was done by the state to halt its decay, and, in 1921, it was declared a historic monument. Not until 1930, though, did the Spanish government begin reconstruction efforts.

A decade later, at the outset of the Second World War, religious life returned to the Abbey, when the state entrusted it to the care of a group of Italian Cistercians.

Today, Santa Maria de Poblet is one of the most extensive remaining medieval abbeys built in the Cistercian style, and nearly all of it has been restored, including the basilica, refectory, cloister, chapter house, scriptorium, abbot's palace, and guest quarters. Only one building near the front gate purposefully remains in a state of ruin, as a sort of permanent memorial to the events which transpired there two centuries ago.

New Vines

In 1989, with the work of restoration nearly complete, the Cistercian monks of Poblet decided to resurrect their winery. It hadn't functioned for over 150 years. They began by once more planting the

Poblet

Pinot Noir that the first monks in Poblet had cultivated. Eventually, to make the best wine possible, the monks decided to partner with winemakers more experienced than themselves and brought in the Codorníu Group to oversee day-to-day operations of the winery.

Over the past decade, under the direction of Codorníu, the monastery vineyards have shifted their focus from growing Pinot Noir to recovering older local varietals, including Trepat, Garrut, and Garnatxa. Grown at a high altitude, in cool locations, the grapes thrive in the Catalonian soils of limestone, clay, and schist. They are then fermented in whole bunches and aged in cement tanks and *foudres*.

Of the more than half dozen wines produced at the monastery, some are single varietal wines. There is a Chardonnay, Pinot Noir, Grenache, and one of the finest wines, the *Abadia de Poblet La Font Voltada*. Made solely from Trepat, it is a dry, balanced red with hints of elderberry, cherry, and white pepper on the palate and a long, silky finish. Serve it with a tagliatelle pasta with ham, peas, and cream, grilled lamb, or a cherry tart for a perfect pairing.

Among the more interesting blends at Poblet is *Abadia de Poblet Tinto*. In it, Trepat, Garrut, and Grenache mingle to create a rich, intense red that is both fruity and floral on the nose and spicy on the palate, with round tannins and a fruity finish. It complements dishes that blend savory with sweet, such as roasted pork tenderloin with a blackberry merlot sauce, bacon-wrapped chicken skewers, or salted caramel brownies.

The *Abadia de Poblet Blanco* is a full, well-balanced white made from a blend of Macabeu and Parellada. The unusual combination results in a wine with wheaty aromas, flavors of melon, white grapefruit, and pineapple, and a smooth, almost creamy finish. It is delicious with roasted turkey, grilled chicken, or a pasta tossed with roasted summer vegetables.

Visiting Santa Maria de Poblet

The Royal Abbey of Santa Maria de Poblet is open to visitors seven days a week. Most tours are in Spanish, but during the busier summer months, English-language tours are offered. Tickets can be purchased at the gate.

The wine cellars are not currently part of the Poblet tour, but all the monastery's wines can be purchased onsite at the monastery shop.

Before or after tours, visitors can lunch at the small café across the street from the monastery. The faithful are also welcome to join the monks for Mass and prayer. Please call the monastery directly to arrange this.

For more information:
E-mail: visita@poblet.cat
Telephone: +34 977 870 089, ext. 275
Website: www.poblet.cat/ca/

Photo Credits

All of the photographs in this book have been generously provided by the vineyards or sourced online as public domain. The exceptions are credited here, with thanks.

Castello di Magione
Daniel Case (licensed under a CC-By-2.0 license), LeDecodeur via Pixabay, and Adrian Michael (licensed under a CC-By-3.0 license).

Abbazia di Monte Oliveto Maggiore
Francesco Giorni and Stacey Box.

Chateau Clos de Vougeot
Serge Chapuy.

Abbaye Sainte-Madeleine du Barroux
Remi Fretille, Odile Pascal, and Christopher Chevallier.

Domaine Laroche
Anna and Michal (licensed under a CC-By-2.0 license).

Bibliography

For the writing of this book, Desmond Seward's classic *Monks and Wine* (New York: Crown, 1979) was an invaluable resource, as was James Hitchcock's *History of the Catholic Church* (San Francisco: Ignatius, 2012) and Warren Carroll's multi-volume series on the history of the Catholic Church, published by Christendom College.

About the Author

Emily Stimpson Chapman is a Catholic wife, mother, and bestselling author of over a dozen books. In addition to her new series of children's books, co-authored with Scott Hahn, her more recent books include *The Story of All Stories: A Bible for Young Catholics*; *Around the Catholic Table: 100+ Simple Recipes for Family and Friends*; *Letters to Myself from the End of World*; *Hope to Die: The Christian Meaning of the Resurrection of the Body*, co-authored with Dr. Scott Hahn; and *The Catholic Table: Finding Joy Where Food and Faith Meet*.

Emily is also the the editor and co-author of the "Formed in Christ" series of high school textbooks; and the author of six studies for the women's ministry Endow.

Over the years, her writing has regularly appeared in *Our Sunday Visitor*, *National Catholic Register*, and *Franciscan Way Magazine*, as well as *First Things*, *Touchstone*, *Faith and Family*, *Lay Witness*, and *Catholic Digest*. She has been honored by both the Catholic Press Association and the Associated Church Press, and was included in Loyola's Best Catholic Writing series.

Emily lives with her husband, Christopher, and their three children in Steubenville, Ohio.

More Pilgrimages from Marian Press

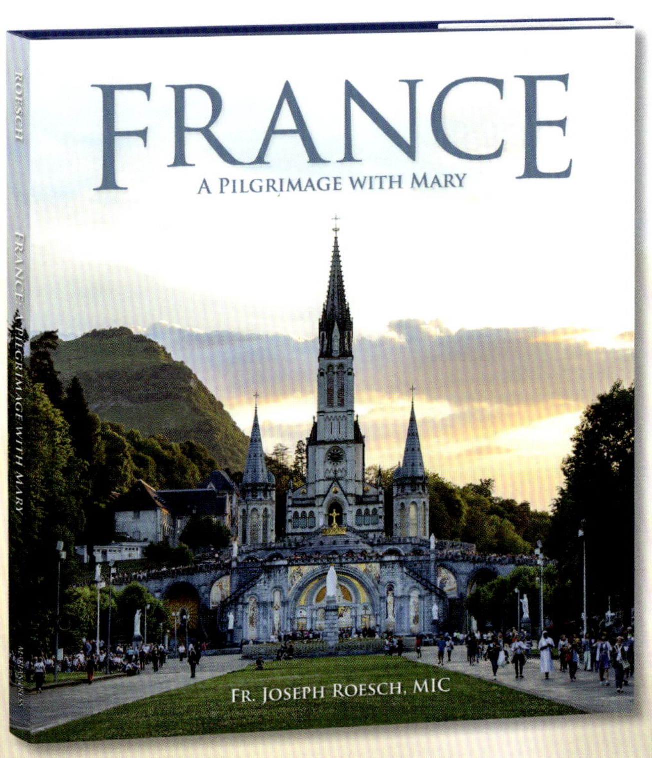

France: A Pilgrimage with Mary

Come along on the journey of a lifetime to the "eldest daughter of the Church": France! This *A Pilgrimage with Mary* immerses you in some of the many shrines, apparition sites, and gorgeous landscapes of France. From Lourdes to Laus, from Rue du Bac to Prouille, journey in spirit across the length and breadth of a land Our Lady has visited many times, discovering a spiritual landscape full of indescribable riches and extraordinary devotions. With the Very Rev. Fr. Joseph Roesch, MIC, as your spiritual director and guide, become immersed in the history of powerful Marian devotions given to us through some of the many French saints, visionaries, and mystics. Rich in beauty and blessings, lavishly illustrated throughout, this book will inspire you to open your heart to Our Lady even more than ever before.
Y131-FRMBK

Visit DivineMercyPlus.org for Fr. Roesch's video tour of France.

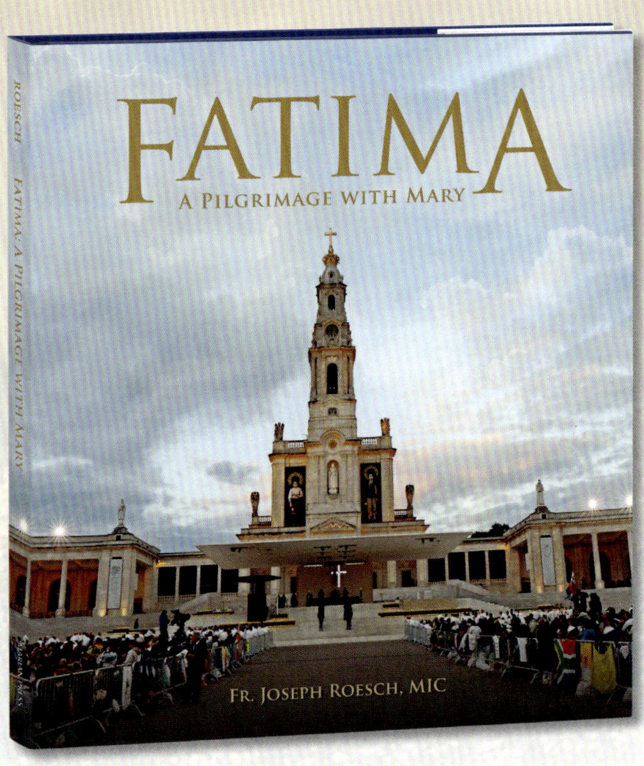

Fatima: A Pilgrimage with Mary

One hundred years ago, three young shepherd children received a visitor from Heaven. That day changed not only their lives, but the lives of people in their village, their country, and the world over. Fatima, a tiny village in Portugal, was the site of these heavenly apparitions. This lavishly illustrated book commemorates the 100th anniversary of the apparitions, and should serve as a reminder to answer Our Lady's call to participate in the salvation of both ourselves and our family in Christ. With over 70 full color and black & white stunning images, this is a wonderful keepsake to commemorate the 100th anniversary of Fatima for a lifetime.
Y131-JRB

Visit DivineMercyPlus.org for Fr. Roesch's video tour of Fatima.

To order, visit ShopMercy.org or call 1-800-462-7426

More Pilgrimages from Marian Press

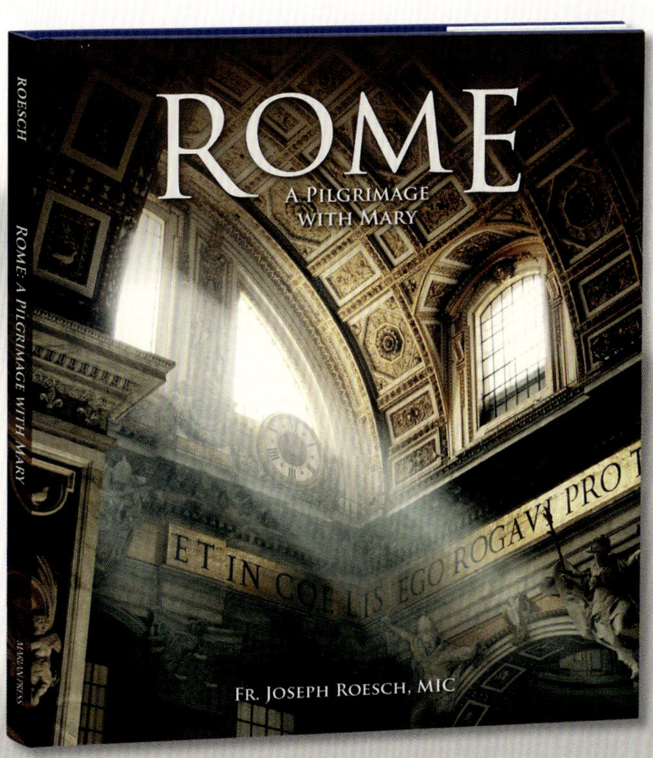

Rome: A Pilgrimage with Mary

Here is another beautifully photographed book by Fr. Joseph Roesch, MIC, that takes the reader on a pictorial "pilgrimage" through the major churches of Rome that are dedicated to Our Blessed Mother. After living in Rome for twelve years, Fr. Joe has come to know and love the many churches of the Eternal City that are either dedicated to or named for the Virgin Mary. Join him as he illuminates the history, art, and human devotion that are associated with these sacred places.

Y131-ROME

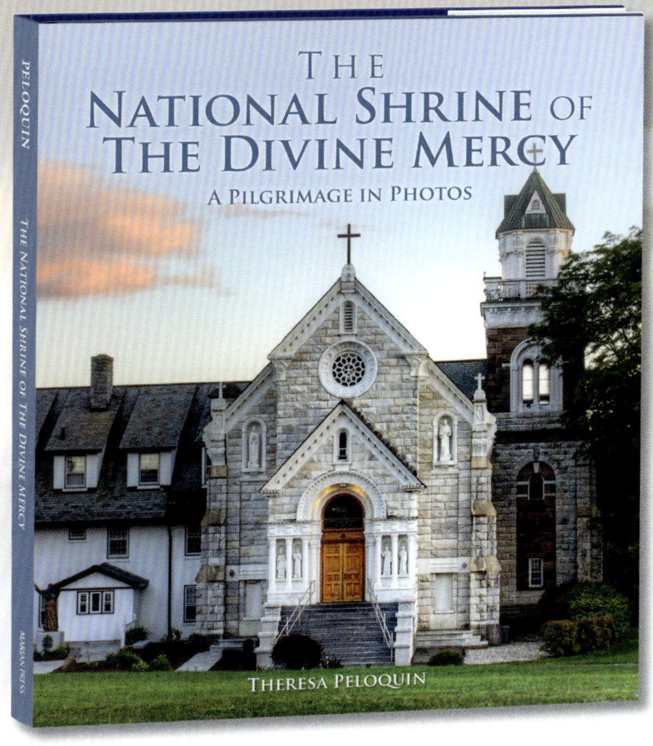

The National Shrine of The Divine Mercy: A Pilgrimage in Photos

The breathtaking grounds of Eden Hill in Stockbridge, Massachusetts, have long been appreciated as a sign of God's mercy in Creation. It's part of the reason the National Shrine of The Divine Mercy — built in thanks for the mercy of God — fits so well here. If you already have come to this holy place, here are images, with text by Theresa Peloquin, to remind you of your pilgrimage. If you are only able to be here in spirit, let these photos speak to your heart, giving you an appreciation for all the Lord has done for His Church through Eden Hill, the Marian Fathers of the Immaculate Conception, and the National Shrine of The Divine Mercy.

Y131-NSDM

To order, visit ShopMercy.org or call 1-800-462-7426